Leading
the Way to
Successful
Volunteer
Involvement

Practical Tools for
Busy Executives

BETTY B. STALLINGS WITH SUSAN J. ELLIS

ENERG!ZE INC.
Especially for **leaders** of volunteers

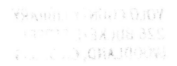

Acknowledgments

My deepest appreciation to Susan J. Ellis, president of Energize, Inc., a mentor, colleague, and friend who encouraged me to write this book and generously shared her wisdom and support throughout the project.

Sincere thanks to Cara Thenot, publications and marketing manager at Energize, Inc., whose keen eye and helpful suggestions were instrumental in enhancing the quality of the book.

To all CEOs and executives who are true champions of volunteer engagement, I applaud and thank you for your helpful contributions to this book and for your belief in the power of volunteers when they are effectively and creatively integrated into organizations and initiatives.

And finally, to all those who lead volunteer engagement with amazing professional skills and passion, I hope this book will be another resource for you to use as you build commitment to the incredible potential of volunteer involvement.

—Betty Stallings

Library of Congress Cataloging-in-Publication Data

Stallings, Betty.
  Leading the way to successful volunteer involvement : practical tools for busy executives / Betty B. Stallings with Susan J. Ellis. -- 1st ed.
    p. cm.
  Includes bibliographical references.
  ISBN 978-0-940576-61-2 (pbk.) -- ISBN 978-0-940576-62-9 (e-book) 1. Voluntarism--Management. 2. Nonprofit organizations--Personnel management. 3. Volunteers. I. Ellis, Susan J. II. Title.
  HN49.V64S73 2010
  658.3--dc22
                    2010031774

Printed in the United States of America

Contents

3 Budgeting for and Funding Volunteer Involvement

4 Hiring and Placing Staff to Lead Volunteer Engagement

5 Creating a Management Team for Volunteer Involvement

6 Building Staff Commitment and Competency to Partner with Volunteers

7 Integrating Volunteers throughout the Organization

8 The Board's Role in Volunteer Engagement

9 Ensuring Legal Compliance and Managing Risk When Involving Volunteers

10 Monitoring, Evaluating, and Improving Volunteer Involvement

Introduction

"If we wish to be all that we can be, we must forever learn better ways to service our mission through volunteers. When it works, it is extraordinary. Volunteers are a cornerstone to this movement. If we wish to keep this pillar strong, we must nurture it with all the resources we can."

Bob Norbie, President and CEO, Special Olympics Montana
Great Falls, Montana

"A volunteer program will not make it if the executive director and management do not walk the talk. Don't bother with a volunteer program unless you truly believe in the value added to your agency. It absolutely must come from the top."

Tina McKenzie, CEO, Six Rivers Planned Parenthood
Eureka, California

In my thirty-five years in the field of volunteerism, I have witnessed stunning and exciting changes in the ways people are donating time to create a better world. However, it is my observation—supported by research in the last decade—that many organizations have not kept up with these changes and therefore are not welcoming, supporting, and empowering community members to be effective advocates and contributors to their missions. Opportunities abound to engage the incredible talents of volunteers, but only if organizations put the infrastructure in place to capture all the time and skills community members can offer.

If you are an executive of a nonprofit or public sector organization, you may fear that *Leading the Way* will add yet another time-consuming responsibility to your overflowing plate. Or you may anticipate a finger wagging, suggesting that you should have known that volunteer involvement needs stronger leadership from the top of the organization. I will try not to do either. I want this book to empower you to take action in ways that perhaps you have not yet considered.

It is highly likely that, despite hours you've spent in classrooms and conference halls, no one has ever effectively articulated to you what is needed to initiate and sustain strategic, outstanding volunteer engagement, particularly from the executive levels of an organization. You no doubt have learned about working with a board of directors, who of course are also volunteers. But too often direct-service and even fundraising volunteers are an afterthought, perhaps buried in a session on human resources. Volunteer management, if considered at all, is seen as a practical function designated to a lower-level staff member. Yet the decisions and policies needed to ensure a strong foundation for community participation require time investment by the top-level executives of an organization.

As an overworked executive, you may not have realized the significant influence that your leadership can have on your organization's volunteer involvement. Or perhaps you have not personally experienced the benefits of a strong, active, and skilled corps of volunteers and thus do not give this part of your organization high priority. Most importantly, there have been very few resources available to guide you in providing the leadership needed to guarantee truly effective volunteer engagement.

The Evolution of New Resources

Susan J. Ellis first tackled this issue in 1986 when she wrote *From the Top Down: The Executive Role in Volunteer Program Success*. The only book ever written specifically for top decision makers about volunteer issues, its unique perspective kept the book a best seller for publisher Energize, Inc. and Susan revised it in 1996. In 2010, noting that almost all the original material still rings true, she updated and expanded a third edition of *From the Top Down* but with a slightly altered subtitle: *The Executive Role in Successful Volunteer Involvement*. The rewording reflects the evolution of thinking that volunteers are not a "program"; they are part of the team of people working toward a mission. You'll find the same language choice in this book.

Having focused on the role of executives for some time myself, I conducted a study in 2005 of twenty-eight executives who already champion volunteer involvement and actively play a role in how volunteers make an impact on delivering the organization's mission. I reported the commonalities of these executives in *12 Key Actions of Volunteer Program Champions: CEOs Who Lead the Way* (downloadable for free at http://www.energizeinc.com/store/5-219-E-1 or http://www.bettystallings.com). Most of the quotations at the start of every section come from the responses of executives to my survey questions.

12 Key Actions was originally meant as a first step to writing a book focused on the role of executive directors in supporting excellence in volunteer involvement. But on further reflection, I realized that the greatest need for busy executives was for a toolkit of practical guides and worksheets for taking immediate action toward strengthening volunteer engagement within their organizations —efficiently, strategically, and successfully.

When I approached publisher Energize, Inc. with my concept, it became obvious that *Leading the Way* should be written as a complement and companion piece to implement the practices discussed in the newest edition of *From the Top Down*. And, to my delight, Susan agreed to assist me in writing this practical resource as she saw it as a natural extension of her book. For your convenience, each section of *Leading the Way* includes a reference to the chapters in *From the Top Down* that explain more fully the concepts on which the tools are based. Conversely, each chapter of *From the Top Down* references the sections of *Leading the Way* that offer the tools to implement the concepts.

Another way that this book complements Susan's is that it avoids the title of "volunteer program manager," although acknowledging that it is one of the many titles in wide use. To reinforce the philosophy that volunteers are not a "program," and to indicate an appropriate degree of responsibility for engaging volunteers *throughout* the organization, you will either see generic language such as "leader of volunteer engagement" or the title that Susan has chosen in *From the Top Down*: "director of volunteer involvement."

Additionally, my CEO volunteer champion study led to the Volunteer Champions Initiative, a research study conducted by Sarah Jane Rehnborg at the RGK Center for Philanthropy and Community Service, The Lyndon B. Johnson School of Public Affairs, The University of Texas at Austin. The focus groups of actual agency executives that Sarah Jane convened made a very strong case for what is needed to invest in volunteer effectiveness. Sarah Jane's 2009 report, *Strategic Volunteer Engagement: a Guide for Nonprofit and Public Sector Leaders* (which features a new Volunteer Involvement Framework™) adds a third companion resource to Susan's and my works.

A Logical Approach

Central to both *Leading the Way* and *From the Top Down* is the belief that the key factor in volunteer success is the attention of an organization's top decision makers. There are no mysteries and few surprises in these pages. Yet few executives take the time to plan and think through what their organization truly wants from volunteer involvement and how they will reach those goals—taking the actions they would naturally take in guiding any other function of the organization. But obviously *you*, by reading this book, are already taking the first step. We want to support you!

Each of the ten sections in *Leading the Way* focuses on one area of strategic volunteer engagement. The sequence is intentional:

Section 1: Personal and Organizational Philosophy about Volunteering

This section shares a process to determine exactly why your organization wants volunteers and how you personally as well as others on your staff view volunteering.

Section 2: Planning for Volunteer Engagement

Based on the beliefs and values about community engagement you define in section one, the next step is conceptualizing and planning how you need and want volunteering to take shape in your organization—integrating and aligning volunteer engagement with the organization's strategic plans/goals.

Section 3: Budgeting for and Funding Volunteer Involvement

Because volunteering is not "free" and the costs need to be understood, this section provides insight about what needs to be funded when involving volunteers and unique tools to help in raising money to cover these costs.

Section 4: Hiring and Placing Staff to Lead Volunteer Engagement

Determining what staff leadership you need and how to find the most competent, enthusiastic person to fill that position are critical factors in ultimate success. Again, uniquely, this section walks you through the process of getting the right leader and options for optimal placement within the organization.

Section 5: Creating a Management Team for Volunteer Involvement

Even a great director of volunteer involvement needs a team representing different areas of the organization to gain the ultimate benefits of engaging volunteers.

Section 6: Building Staff Commitment and Competency to Partner with Volunteers

Your staff may be highly educated and provide outstanding service to clients, but often they have not been trained in partnering with volunteers to accomplish the work. This section helps you to assess staff skill level and attitudes about community participation and explores methods to support and recognize staff who work with volunteers.

Section 7: Integrating Volunteers throughout the Organization

This section considers how *every* function or department of your organization relates to volunteer involvement and provides guidelines for expanding everyone's horizons about ways that volunteers can contribute at all levels and in all activities of the organization. Much of this material has never been articulated in print before.

Section 8: The Board's Role in Volunteer Engagement

The board definitely *has* a role! This section identifies why boards must be informed and supportive of their organization's volunteer engagement and shares various methods of communication to make sure this happens.

Section 9: Ensuring Legal Compliance and Managing Risk When Involving Volunteers

We live in litigious times and, while volunteering is not inherently riskier than any other activity, it is imperative to ensure the safety of everyone connected to your organization. This section helps you consider the volunteer-related legal and risk issues that deserve your attention.

Section 10: Monitoring, Evaluating, and Improving Volunteer Involvement

This last section brings you full circle back to examining your philosophy of volunteerism and shares methods to evaluate the success of your goals and objectives in engaging volunteers in your organization.

Bibliography and Other Volunteerism Resources

References and Web links indicate where you can turn for more information on laying the foundation and supporting volunteer involvement.

The Tools in this Book

To help you recognize the different types of tools in this book, each is identified with an icon and header. The types of tools you'll find in each section include:

Introduction to the Executive Role: This is a brief explanation of how your role can contribute to the success of volunteer work, and it includes a reference to the chapters of *From the Top Down* that cover this material more fully.

 Idea Stimulator: Material presented to guide you in thinking (or re-thinking) about key issues related to supporting volunteer involvement.

 Action Steps: A suggested sequence of actions to implement a volunteer engagement goal.

 Checklist: A list of actions or items to check off after completing or assembling, or as a reminder before acting.

 Key Concept: Information useful as the context for using the other tools in a section, which may include background material or useful resources.

 Example: Samples of statements, letters, forms, and more from actual organizations, shared as excellent models for you in developing your own versions.

 Worksheet: A reflection or planning tool that is either a sequence of questions or a grid or table to complete. Worksheets are formatted with space to record responses or decisions, and therefore can be copied and distributed to others involved in a planning session.

 Self-Inquiry: A list of statements to score or questions to which you respond to evaluate or assess current ideas or conditions.

 Survey: A form you can distribute, as is, to gather responses from others in your organization.

 Collaboration Strategy: Used specifically in section seven for exploring the potential interrelationships of volunteer resources and other functions in the organization.

 Executive Self-Assessment: Concludes each section, giving you a list of the actions needed by an executive from which you can gauge your own involvement in this management area.

Using the Tools

It is my hope that you will find these tools helpful to you as executive and to the rest of your organization's management staff, whether paid or volunteer.

Because volunteer engagement initiatives and the staffing of them vary so much, the director of volunteer involvement may be the person who initially takes these tools, modifies them, and makes them available to executives. Even if this is how the process starts, ultimately top decision makers must take responsibility for their role in assuring success.

Having been a nonprofit executive director for fourteen years, I remember continually being concerned about generating resources (people and funds) to support our mission. I learned that supporting effective volunteer engagement was one of the key ways to accomplish that mission. The tools in *Leading the Way* are what I wish someone had brought to me to guide and enhance my efforts back then—and I hope they fill the gap for today's organization leaders.

An executive in one of my audiences recently said, *"Bring me a resource that begins to solve problems I lose sleep over and my door is open!"* I hope *your* door is open!

Betty B. Stallings
Pleasanton, CA
August 2010

section

1

Personal and Organizational Philosophy about Volunteering

To stay viable in the nonprofit sector, I believe you must invest in bringing communities of people into the work you do. Those non-profit organizations who do this through volunteers will rise to the top of their sector. People want to be part of something, and if they are, they will support you, advocate for you and build alliances for you. This also changes how you do business because you are truly bringing in people with different backgrounds that will keep you re-thinking the way you do business, which is a very healthy thing. You must invest resources, both financial and staff to make this happen.

June Koegel, President and CEO
Volunteers of America
Northern New England
Brunswick, Maine

The philosophy of the volunteer program states that volunteers complement, assist and partner with the paid staff in virtually every facet of the museum. We value this contribution and hope to offer each volunteer a satisfying, productive and rewarding experience.

Sandi Yoder, President and CEO
Living History Farms
Urbandale, Iowa

CONTENTS

CONCEPTS IN DEPTH

The tools in this section apply the concepts discussed at length in the book, *From the Top Down: The Executive Role in Successful Volunteer Involvement*, 3rd edition, by Susan J. Ellis (Philadelphia: Energize, Inc., 2010), specifically:

- **Introduction: Needed Executive Attention**
- **Chapter 1: Why Volunteers?**

Introduction to the Executive Role

Executives can have a great impact by initiating and leading a discussion throughout their organizations to create a *statement of philosophy on volunteer engagement*. It can also be called a *value* or *commitment* statement. Such a document clarifies the rationale and value of volunteers to the organization and makes the commitment to community participation clear to everyone.

Many of the most supportive executives in my study, *12 Key Actions of Volunteer Program Champions: CEOs Who Lead the Way* (2005), indicated that they had not thought of the significance of creating a philosophy statement regarding volunteer engagement. After thinking through its implications for enhancing the mission, they all asked for a process to create one and for some real-life examples from other organizations.

A written statement of philosophy expresses a core set of values and beliefs about volunteers for executive leadership and staff—one which does not change as people come and go. An established organizational statement about the value and role of volunteers also encourages consistent support of volunteer engagement throughout the whole organization, rather than enabling the individual philosophies and biases of every department manager and staff member to create dissonant beliefs about the value of volunteers. Once developed, the statement should be put in *writing* to ensure employees, volunteers, funders, and the public know what it is.

As executive director, your personal philosophy and values about volunteer involvement are integral to the ultimate success of your organization's volunteer engagement strategy. So, this section begins with tools for exploring your personal history of volunteering, both in being a volunteer yourself and in managing volunteers. These tools also give you an opportunity to explore your current assumptions about volunteers and the impact of these assumptions on your leadership in supporting a strong commitment to volunteerism.

Your work in engaging the board of directors, legislators, or others with authority over your strategic plan for involving volunteers is crucial. Your and the board's support for this plan will be the ultimate test of whether the philosophy is living-in-action throughout the organization. Executive vision, attention, enthusiasm, and desire to hold all employees, including top management, to a standard of excellence when working with volunteers will make the difference in whether volunteer contributions reach maximum potential in your organization.

> *"...your personal philosophy and values about volunteer involvement are integral to the ultimate success of your organization's volunteer engagement strategy."*

INSTRUCTIONS FOR

Worksheet: Personal Volunteer History

Purpose:

The following worksheet is designed to help you remember and reflect on the volunteer activities you have done personally throughout your life— some of which you may not have considered to be "volunteering."

The worksheet can also be used in a group setting—with a management team, for example. The discussion of everyone's responses will demonstrate:

- That everyone has at least some personal volunteer experience

- How diverse volunteering is in our society

- That personal volunteer experience impacts each person's philosophy on volunteer engagement in various contexts

Process:

1. Complete the *Worksheet* on the next page yourself or distribute it to a group to complete individually.

   - Note that people often do not identify all the activities they do without pay as "volunteering." So it's important to get all respondents to think hard about the type of service they've done.

   - Suggest they think of what they might label as a class or youth group project, an internship, pro bono service, lay ministry, political action, neighborliness, and other similar terms.

2. Then consider the reflection questions on page 11 for yourself or with the group.

Personal Volunteer History

Think back to different times in your life and identify some ways you "volunteered," "helped in the community," "served others," or did anything to assist a cause for which you were not paid a wage. How have these experiences of volunteering and any experiences you have had in supervising/partnering with volunteers influenced your personal philosophy of the value (or potential value) of volunteers?

Stage of Life	What you did:	What did you call it? Why did you do it?
Before age 5 *(maybe with your family)*		
In elementary school *(maybe with your class)*		
In high school		
As a university student		

Stage of Life	In your personal and family life *(include what you do on behalf of a member of your family or your neighborhood, things you like to do as recreation, etc.)*	In your business or professional life *(include professional society activities, community boards, etc.)*	What did you call it? Why did you do it?
In your 20s			
In your 30s and 40s			
In your 50s and 60s			
In your 70s and beyond			

(continued)

Personal Volunteer History
(continued)

Now reflect on your life history of volunteering:

1. Were you surprised at the amount and range of the things you've done in your life (whether a lot or a little) that could be labeled "volunteering"?

    _____

    _____

2. Which of your personal volunteer experiences were the most memorable, valuable, or rewarding for you? Why?

    _____

    _____

3. Which did you dislike or feel wasted your time? Why?

    _____

    _____

4. What is your memory of some of your volunteer experiences as they relate to:

    a. How you were recruited to carry out the work

    _____

    _____

    b. How welcoming the organization was

    _____

    _____

    c. How well the organization oriented you and prepared you for the work you agreed to do

    _____

    _____

    d. How flexible they were with your time availability

    _____

    _____

(continued)

Personal Volunteer History
(continued)

e. Whether you had input into the way things were organized and the positions you held

_____

_____

f. How well the organization showed appreciation for your contributions of time

_____

_____

5. Which activities do you feel made the greatest contribution to the person, organization or cause you were trying to help? (Did any make things worse?)

_____

_____

6. How do your answers to the previous questions give you an understanding of how to treat volunteers in your organization?

_____

_____

7. What has been your past experience in supervising/partnering with volunteers as it relates to:

a. The impact that the volunteers had on the organization's mission

_____

_____

b. The skills and dedication that volunteers shared with the organization

_____

_____

c. The organizational support needed to foster excellence in volunteer involvement

_____

_____

(continued)

Personal Volunteer History
(continued)

8. As a result of your experience of being a volunteer yourself and of supervising other volunteers, what is your current feeling about the value of volunteer engagement?

   _____

   _____

9. How do these feelings influence your role in guiding and supporting volunteer engagement within your organization?

   _____

   _____

What Are My Beliefs about Volunteering?

(Note: There are no "right" answers, but the questions are worth considering and will impact your leadership of volunteer involvement.)

- Why is volunteering important to society as a whole? Are there any negatives?

- Why is volunteering important to my organization? Are there any negatives?

- Why is volunteering important to the individuals who volunteer? Are there any negatives?

- What do I see as the purpose of my role as an executive or senior manager as it relates to involving volunteers in our organization?

- How do I define "volunteer"?

- Are there other words I use (or even prefer) over the word "volunteer"?

- Is there anything I feel a volunteer should not be asked to do? (Why?)

- What is my feeling about the variety of "mandates" for doing service? (Court related, school requirements, etc.)

- Do valuable gifts and stipends ever cross the line into "low pay" and change volunteering somehow?

- Is volunteering a right or a privilege?

- Do I agree that "any volunteering is a political act"?

- What do I see as the relationship of work-for-pay and volunteering? How do I respond to labor union arguments against volunteering as "taking paid jobs"?

- What is (or should be) the connection between all-volunteer associations and agency-based volunteer "programs"?

- What is the relationship between giving time and giving money?

- What is the balance between my loyalty to the support of volunteers and my obligations to my organization and the clients we serve?

INSTRUCTIONS FOR

Self-Inquiry: The Value of Volunteers
for Our Organization

Purpose:

Prior to developing your organization's philosophy or commitment to volunteers, it is useful to consider the value that volunteers currently bring to the organization versus your desired impact of volunteer engagement. This *Self-Inquiry* guides such an assessment for yourself or for a group of people in your organization who are assessing the current situation prior to the development of a philosophy statement.

Process:

1. Complete the form on the next page yourself and/or distribute it to a group of selected staff and volunteers asking each to fill it in independently. Having representation from different stakeholders (as well as a mix of newcomers and longtime workers) will help you uncover consistency or variation in viewpoints throughout the organization. It also ensures that the findings will be analyzed objectively.

2. For each of the twelve asset statements, indicate your response to the statement by placing an X on each of two scales indicating:

   - How desirable you think the asset is/could be to your organization

   - The degree to which the asset is currently a reality in your organization

3. Discuss the responses:

   - Is there a significant discrepancy between what is desirable and what is reality in your organization? Why? What can you do about it?

   - What other benefits and values does your organization derive or could it derive from volunteer contributions?

   - If several staff members and volunteers have filled out the form, are there statements on which they differed significantly in their assessments? Why?

   - Is there a consistent, shared philosophy of volunteer engagement within your organization?

The Value of Volunteers for Our Organization

Below is a list of benefits that volunteers potentially bring to an organization.

Place an X on each of the two scales to indicate:

4. Whether you agree or disagree that the value is desired by your organization

5. Whether this value is a reality for your organization

1. **Effectively engaged volunteers become the best ambassadors/most credible spokespersons for our organization in the community.**

Desirable: _____
       Strongly disagree   *Strongly agree*

Reality: _____
       Not at all   *Always*

2. **Volunteers reduce staff workloads.**

Desirable: _____
       Strongly disagree   *Strongly agree*

Reality: _____
       Not at all   *Always*

3. **Volunteers expand our services and help to fulfill our mission.**

Desirable: _____
       Strongly disagree   *Strongly agree*

Reality: _____
       Not at all   *Always*

4. **Volunteers bring an outside perspective, wisdom, and experience into our organization.**

Desirable: _____
       Strongly disagree   *Strongly agree*

Reality: _____
       Not at all   *Always*

(continued)

The Value of Volunteers for Our Organization
(continued)

5. **Involved volunteers become financial donors to the organization.**

   Desirable: _____

   Strongly disagree   *Strongly agree*

   Reality: _____

   Not at all   *Always*

6. **Volunteers bring diversity and create inclusiveness.**

   Desirable: _____

   Strongly disagree   *Strongly agree*

   Reality: _____

   Not at all   *Always*

7. **Volunteers bring energy and moral support as well as new ideas and perspectives to our organization and the issues we face.**

   Desirable: _____

   Strongly disagree   *Strongly agree*

   Reality: _____

   Not at all   *Always*

8. **Volunteers bring new skills and expertise not necessarily available from the current staff.**

   Desirable: _____

   Strongly disagree   *Strongly agree*

   Reality: _____

   Not at all   *Always*

9. **Volunteers are catalysts for new program development and testing out new ideas.**

   Desirable: _____

   Strongly disagree   *Strongly agree*

   Reality: _____

   Not at all   *Always*

(continued)

The Value of Volunteers for Our Organization

(continued)

10. **Volunteers build alliances and connections between us and their outside circle of contacts, such as businesses, faith communities, organizations and associations—and bring those resources to us when needed.**

   Desirable: _____
   Strongly disagree   *Strongly agree*

   Reality: _____
   Not at all   *Always*

11. **Volunteers are advocates for our cause in multiple arenas because they are private citizens and voters.**

   Desirable: _____
   Strongly disagree   *Strongly agree*

   Reality: _____
   Not at all   *Always*

12. **Volunteers are community watchdogs for responsible use of donated time and funds.**

   Desirable: _____
   Strongly disagree   *Strongly agree*

   Reality: _____
   Not at all   *Always*

Creating a Statement of Philosophy on Volunteer Engagement

What is a statement of philosophy on volunteer engagement?

It's a written document that articulates an organization's belief in the value and role that volunteers play in carrying out its mission. This statement is then shared throughout the organization and with the public, becoming the foundation upon which volunteer engagement rests. It can also be called a value statement or a commitment statement.

What is its purpose?

How volunteers are perceived in an organization is reflected, intentionally or unintentionally, by the type of volunteer assignments created, the amount and type of resources allocated to engaging volunteers, and the credibility given to volunteer input. Having a statement of philosophy that is understood by all stakeholders (employees, managers, executives, board members, etc.) of the organization makes the difference between "using" volunteers and "engaging" volunteers as partners, effectively and productively, in carrying out the mission. Stating the value and role of volunteers:

- Expresses the organization's commitment to volunteers.

- Establishes a clear relationship between staff and volunteers.

- Creates a framework upon which the board can develop goals and policies for the organization's volunteer engagement.

- Gives clear direction to all staff that they are expected to partner with volunteers.

- Becomes the fundamental principle that will guide the organization in developing a vision for volunteer engagement at its best.

- Helps to determine whether prospective staff and volunteers are a good fit for the organization.

- Ensures that the organization's commitment to volunteer involvement does not change with trends or new executive staff.

- Helps volunteers understand their value to the organization.

Who can (should) be involved in deliberating and determining the statement of philosophy on volunteers in an organization?

Creating, reviewing or enhancing your organization's statement of philosophy can be initiated at the top or in the middle of an organization. Ultimately, the final philosophy must be embraced by the board and executive(s) to have clout in setting a standard of approach.

Creating a Statement of Philosophy on Volunteer Engagement

Step 1

With key staff, board members and other volunteers, discuss the question, "If we had all the money we want and need to support the organization's mission, would we still utilize volunteers and WHY?"

This tough question is posed by Susan Ellis in her book, *From the Top Down* (2010, 13-26). Spending time thinking through an answer is a way to get at the true value of volunteers beyond the usual—and inaccurate—response that they merely "save" money.

Step 2

Revisit the mission of your organization.

Basically, the mission is the purpose for which the agency exists. It is not a list of what you do but is rather a declaration of what you want to accomplish (e.g., eradicate hunger in our community, end violence among our youth). Being clear about the organization's mission is critical to deciding how volunteers will be involved to support that mission.

Step 3

Identify how you involve volunteers today in carrying out your mission.

Answer these questions:

- Who is defined as a volunteer in our organization?

- What do they do?

- Do they have a wide range of roles, including program support, consulting, short-term projects, research and advocacy, administrative support, fund-raising, etc.?

- Do they work throughout the organization, in all departments and units, and partner with everyone from frontline staff to executives?

- Are volunteers considered partners in our work or assistants and helpers? (These are key words that set the tone for how volunteers are perceived.)

(continued)

Creating a Statement of Philosophy
on Volunteer Engagement

(continued)

- Are there any activities from which volunteers are barred due to concerns about confidentiality, risk, or staff resistance? (Revisit any of these as they may be based on outdated or inappropriate criteria.)

- How do staff view the involvement of volunteers? Do they have personal biases or stereotypes that might cause resistance, or are they open to the different ways volunteers might contribute?

Step 4

Re-examine the questions above, but this time create a vision of potentially great volunteer engagement.

Have executives, staff, board and volunteers give input envisioning their hopes and wishes for how your organization might more successfully involve volunteers in the future. Discuss the impact this could have on your mission. Don't be concerned about why you don't currently have volunteer involvement at this level—just visualize an expanded corps of volunteers serving the organization, effectively and creatively, in myriad ways.

Step 5

Identify your key stakeholders (internal and external) who do or could benefit and/or contribute to successful volunteer engagement.

Include their input into the discussion of the organization's philosophy or value statement about volunteers.

Step 6

Based on your answers in steps 1-5, develop a draft of a statement of philosophy on volunteer engagement for review and discussion by all stakeholders. Rewrite the draft until the statement accurately reflects your collective values.

Here is a sample philosophy statement offered in *From the Top Down*:

Our agency encourages the teamwork of employees and volunteers so that we can offer our consumers the best services possible. Volunteers contribute their

(continued)

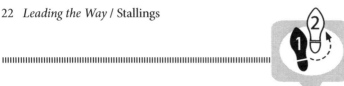

Creating a Statement of Philosophy on Volunteer Engagement
(continued)

unique talents, skills, and knowledge of our community to provide personalized attention to clients, enable the paid staff to concentrate on the work for which they were trained, and educate the public about our organization and its cause. (Ellis 2010, 28)

More examples are on the next pages.

Step 7

Ask the board of directors to formally approve the statement of philosophy to make it an official part of the culture and policies of the organization.

Step 8

Disseminate the statement of philosophy widely to make certain that it becomes a living philosophy guiding the organization's engagement of volunteers.

Consider all the ways you can share the statement, such as:

• Put on a plaque and hang in the lobby

• Include at staff and volunteer orientation and training sessions

• Put in policy and procedure manuals

• Include on your Web site

• Share regularly at departmental staff meetings

• Mention at volunteer recognition events

• Include in materials that go out to the public, such as letterhead, recruitment flyers, pamphlets, monthly newsletters, etc.

Step 9

Review the statement annually to determine if the organization is continuing to be guided by this philosophy/commitment statement.

EXAMPLE

Sample Statements of Philosophy from Various Organizations

Carlsbad City Library
Carlsbad
CA

Carlsbad City Library is best served by providing citizens fulfilling opportunities to utilize their skills to enhance the quest for knowledge and the enjoyment of reading in the community. Citizen engagement is a major part of the library.

We believe that citizen engagement:

- *Improves customer service and our relationship with the community we serve*

- *Allows the library to expand our capacity and enhance our services*

- *Provides us with the community's point of view and takes back to the community word of our services*

We are committed to the recruitment, training and support of citizen volunteers to ensure their continued involvement in library services and to develop this resource to its fullest.

Thanks to Sue Irey, Community Volunteer Coordinator, City of Carlsbad

Chabot Space and Science Center
Oakland
CA

Volunteer Guiding Principles

- *Volunteers will experience a friendly, helpful and educational environment in which to contribute their full range of talents, skills and experience.*

- *Volunteers will find opportunities for personal growth and development as they contribute to the excellence inherent in Chabot programs.*

- *Volunteers will be supported and recognized for their creative and effective partnerships with each other, staff, Chabot partners and constituents.*

- *Volunteers and staff will have an ongoing, reciprocal exchange of information and ideas to best accomplish our goals.*

- *Training, support and rewards will be given to staff for successful involvement of volunteers.*

Thanks to Megan Gray, Manager of Volunteer Services, Chabot Space and Science Center

(continued)

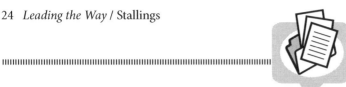

Sample Statements of Philosophy
from Various Organizations

(continued)

Planned Parenthood Mar Monte

San Jose CA

Philosophy of Volunteer and Intern Involvement

Planned Parenthood Mar Monte has a long history of volunteer and intern involvement and is committed to providing a rewarding and satisfying experience that offers opportunities for social and intellectual enrichment and personal growth. Volunteers and interns are an integral part of Planned Parenthood Mar Monte and allow us to provide a level of service to the community that would otherwise be impossible.

http://www.plannedparenthood.org/mar-monte/volunteers-interns-4774.htm

National Multiple Sclerosis Society (NMSS)

The Philosophy for Volunteerism in NMSS:

Volunteers are integral partners in the fight against multiple sclerosis. Volunteers across the country contribute resources – time, knowledge, skills and leadership – that infuse the organization with energy and passion that will end the devastating effects of multiple sclerosis.

The Vision for Volunteerism in NMSS:

The National Multiple Sclerosis Society strives to be known and respected for excellence in volunteerism among the country's voluntary health agencies. We see an organization where volunteers work as partners at all levels, and where their contributions are embraced, valued and recognized. Volunteer involvement will be expanded and enhanced through exemplary training programs and tools. Our organization will welcome the diversity that volunteers bring to our work and is committed to providing growth and development for those who choose to contribute their resources.

The National Multiple Sclerosis Society is enriched by a large network of volunteers who are excited by their work and empowered to achieve the mission of the organization.

(continued)

Sample Statements of Philosophy
from Various Organizations

(continued)

Alberta
Children's
Hospital
Calgary
Alberta

Statement of Commitment to the Volunteer

The Alberta Children's Hospital recognizes the contribution of volunteers in assisting staff to fulfill the mission of the hospital. Towards the continued pursuit of excellence in volunteerism and in support of volunteers as valued members of the ACH team, the hospital's administration makes the following commitment to the volunteer community at ACH.

1. *The hospital will support a Volunteer Resources Department providing appropriate staffing to manage the volunteer program.*

2. *Hospital staff, both professional and support, who are directing volunteers will be oriented to the needs of volunteers. In specific terms, all new staff, as part of their orientation, will receive instruction from Volunteer Resources. All staff working with volunteers will receive ongoing education from Volunteer Resources as required.*

3. *Hospital staff will play a role in the orientation, directing, evaluation and recognition of volunteers working in their areas.*

4. *Staff will facilitate a positive environment for volunteers working in their areas. This will involve welcoming them, assisting them, mentoring them when necessary and thanking them regularly for their contribution.*

5. *Staff working with volunteers will be recognized for this contribution.*

Signed by the Administrative Leaders of the Alberta Children's Hospital and the Regional Senior Operating Officers.

Valeriote, Terry. (1999). "Building Commitment for the Volunteer Program: A Replicable Model." *The Journal of Volunteer Administration*, XVII, 2, Winter 1999, 25-29.

(continued)

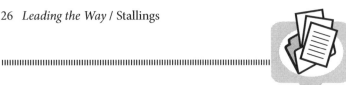

Sample Statements of Philosophy
from Various Organizations

(continued)

Spokane County Juvenile Court

Spokane WA

The Spokane County Juvenile Court is committed to providing the best and most appropriate services possible. To realize this goal, our Department shall make every effort to enlist the cooperation of all available resources. The Department is committed to the development of a public/private partnership which includes volunteers as an important and necessary ingredient in the development and delivery of services.

In addition to the above, our Department plans to actively implement and maintain a responsible program of citizen involvement because:

1. *Our Department will never have sufficient resources to meet all service needs. Even if such resources were available (professional staff, finances, facilities, etc.), the Department would still believe it necessary for the community to become involved in juvenile issues.*

2. *It has been demonstrated repeatedly that volunteers can significantly enhance, expand and upgrade services. With appropriate recruitment, screening, training, and supervision, volunteers can perform almost any task effectively and responsibly.*

3. *The Department feels it necessary to involve the community in the problems we are trying to alleviate or solve. Efforts to involve the community in organization affairs will help to educate the public about these problems and will create a more enlightened and active citizenry. Because volunteers are regarded as key members of the Juvenile Court team, their increased involvement in our Department will be pursued.*

Making the Statement of Philosophy
a Living Document

- How will we disseminate the statement of philosophy?

  _____

  _____

- What roles will be played by the board, executive director, director of volunteer involvement, and other key leaders/stakeholders in the dissemination of the statement?

  _____

  _____

- In what official documents and ongoing training does this statement need to be included?

  _____

  _____

- How will we assure that the statement of philosophy serves as a guide for:
  - Determining the types and range of positions that volunteers can hold in the organization?

    _____

    _____

  - Hiring new staff and setting expectations of all staff to partner with volunteers?

    _____

    _____

  - Allocating resources and support to ensure that we demonstrate the agency's commitment to volunteers?

    _____

    _____

  - Developing policies and procedures for volunteer involvement?

    _____

    _____

(continued)

Making the Statement of Philosophy
a Living Document
(continued)

- Explaining to volunteers how and why they are contributing to the work of the organization?

  _____

  _____

- How can we ensure that the statement of philosophy is visible to all, understood as part of our organizational culture, and reviewed periodically?

  _____

  _____

  _____

Do I create and support a strong philosophy of volunteer engagement with these actions?

1. I have explored my personal philosophy of volunteer engagement to determine its influence on the support I give to my organization's engagement of volunteers.

   ☐ Yes   ☐ No   ☐ Sometimes   ☐ Will now initiate   ☐ Not relevant

2. I have involved the board of directors in the creation and support of an organizational volunteer philosophy statement expressing our values in volunteer engagement.

   ☐ Yes   ☐ No   ☐ Sometimes   ☐ Will now initiate   ☐ Not relevant

3. I work together with appropriate staff to envision strong, high-return-on-investment volunteer engagement to support the mission of our organization.

   ☐ Yes   ☐ No   ☐ Sometimes   ☐ Will now initiate   ☐ Not relevant

4. When appropriate I give helpful feedback as to how to diminish barriers keeping our organization from having the best volunteer involvement possible.

   ☐ Yes   ☐ No   ☐ Sometimes   ☐ Will now initiate   ☐ Not relevant

5. I serve in a volunteer capacity in another organization to sensitize myself to the environment and support volunteers need to be successful.

   ☐ Yes   ☐ No   ☐ Sometimes   ☐ Will now initiate   ☐ Not relevant

6. I network with other CEOs who place a strong value on volunteerism and discuss how to maximize volunteer benefits for our mission.

   ☐ Yes   ☐ No   ☐ Sometimes   ☐ Will now initiate   ☐ Not relevant

7. In speaking engagements, I enthusiastically share the impact that volunteers have on the mission of our organization.

   ☐ Yes   ☐ No   ☐ Sometimes   ☐ Will now initiate   ☐ Not relevant

8. I hold all members of the organization accountable to living up to the organization's philosophy of volunteer engagement.

   ☐ Yes   ☐ No   ☐ Sometimes   ☐ Will now initiate   ☐ Not relevant

(continued)

Do I create and support a strong philosophy of volunteer engagement with these actions?

(continued)

9. I help to disseminate the volunteer philosophy to all staff and volunteers.

    ☐ Yes   ☐ No   ☐ Sometimes   ☐ Will now initiate   ☐ Not relevant

10. I work with appropriate staff to make certain that the philosophy is shared with all new staff, is present in our policies and procedures and staff training, is included on our Web site and is continually visible to all volunteers and guests who come to our offices.

    ☐ Yes   ☐ No   ☐ Sometimes   ☐ Will now initiate   ☐ Not relevant

11. I am continually expanding my awareness of the potential value of volunteer partners in our mission.

    ☐ Yes   ☐ No   ☐ Sometimes   ☐ Will now initiate   ☐ Not relevant

Planning for Volunteer Engagement

> *"Cultivation of volunteers cannot be a "fit in" activity. It must be part of the organization's plan."*

Arlyn A. White, President and CEO
National Multiple Sclerosis Society
Central New England Chapter
Waltham, Massachusetts

> *The volunteer program is included in our public feedback sessions as well as part of the organization's strategic plan.*

Genie Zakrzewski, President and CEO
Leroy Springs and Co., Inc.
Fort Mill, South Carolina

CONTENTS

- **Introduction** to the Executive Role

- **Worksheet:** Questions to Answer Before Planning (or Redesigning) Volunteer Involvement

- **Checklist:** Organizational Readiness to Engage Volunteers or Expand Volunteer Involvement

- **Action Steps:** Planning a Volunteer Involvement Strategy

- **Action Steps:** Integrating Volunteer Engagement into Organizational Strategic Planning

- **Action Steps:** Align/Create Volunteer Positions in Response to Strategic Organizational Goals

- **Idea Stimulator:** A Starting Point for Forming Policies Related to Volunteers

- **Example:** Volunteer Policies and Procedures

- **Executive Self-Assessment:** *Do I plan for volunteer involvement and develop appropriate policies with these actions?*

CONCEPTS IN DEPTH

The tools in this section apply the concepts discussed at length in the book, *From the Top Down: The Executive Role in Successful Volunteer Involvement,* 3rd edition, by Susan J. Ellis (Philadelphia: Energize, Inc., 2010), specifically:

- Chapter 2: Considerations in Planning

Introduction to the Executive Role

As with all elements of a well-run organization, careful planning for volunteer involvement will strengthen the ultimate impact volunteers will make. Yet too often volunteer participation evolves without much attention from the organization's decision makers. The result? Without initial and ongoing planning for volunteer engagement, even the most skilled volunteer management staff won't be able to help volunteers contribute their maximum potential. For example, other staff may resist working with volunteers, volunteer management staff may be unaware of an area in the organization that desperately needs volunteer help, highly skilled volunteers may waste their time in the wrong role, or staff could go into crisis mode when not trained to work with volunteers who show up on their doorstep.

Not only is it vital to have strategic planning sessions about volunteer involvement itself, but volunteer engagement also needs to be a significant factor in strategic planning for the entire organization. How will volunteers contribute to all new initiatives? to new client needs? to moving in new directions? Part of planning is considering available resources; volunteers are one aspect of your resource mix, as important as funds and employees.

In any organizational planning, the leader of volunteer involvement should be at the table to offer both the potential and the constraints of the corps of unpaid workers. Further, both frontline staff and volunteers should participate in the planning process at some level so that they buy in to the plan and support the roles volunteers will play in achieving the organization's mission.

This chapter focuses on the significance of careful initial planning of volunteer engagement in an organization and the significant tie between the organization's strategic planning and volunteer involvement. It also provides tools to develop policies and procedures related to involving volunteers—an important part of planning that executives and the board of directors are responsible for overseeing.

The executive director can do the following:

- Make certain that initial planning (or re-designing) of volunteer engagement is done strategically and realistically.

- Remember to include planning for volunteer participation in any preparation for new projects, services, or campaigns.

- Ensure that volunteers and the person designated to lead volunteer involvement are actively contributing to the organization's strategic planning process.

- Focus on the outcome and impact of volunteer activity when establishing goals.

- Ensure that volunteer positions, just as paid staff jobs, are designed to work toward the organization's mission and established goals.

- Contribute to and oversee the development of volunteer policies and procedures to ensure safe and productive volunteer engagement.

> *"...volunteer engagement also needs to be a significant factor in strategic planning for the entire organization."*

Questions to Answer before Planning (or Redesigning) Volunteer Involvement

*Before responding to the questions below, review the organization's **mission statement**. Then review the **statement of philosophy of volunteer involvement** that you developed in the previous section—or go back and develop one. These documents lay the foundation for the planning that follows.*

1. Who has a stake in creating or strengthening our volunteer involvement and, therefore, should be involved in planning for it?

   _____

   _____

2. How can volunteers contribute to meeting our organization's mission, strategies, and goals?

   _____

   _____

3. What type of volunteers do we most want to attract (consider backgrounds, age, ethnicity, professions, etc.)? Why?

   _____

   _____

4. What specific roles do we see volunteers playing in our organization and what do we expect volunteers to accomplish?

   _____

   _____

5. What policies and procedures must be developed or revised to give operational support to volunteer engagement?

   _____

   _____

6. Who will lead our volunteer engagement effort and where will the position be placed in the organization? What is our rationale for these decisions?

   _____

   _____

(continued)

Questions to Answer before Planning
(or Redesigning) Volunteer Involvement
(continued)

7. What resources (financial and in-kind) do we have or will we generate to support volunteer engagement?

    _____

    _____

8. Are staff committed to and competent in partnering with volunteers? Will we need to work through any staff resistance? What training will we need to provide to staff who partner with volunteers?

    _____

    _____

9. How will planning for volunteers be integrated with overall agency planning?

    _____

    _____

Organizational Readiness to Engage Volunteers or Expand Volunteer Involvement

☐ We have identified all the people who already volunteer with us now, including members of the board of directors or advisory councils, student interns, civic groups who help at events, episodic and seasonal volunteers (such as Make a Difference Day participants, holiday banquet volunteers), and anyone else who contributes their time and talent without receiving pay.

☐ We have asked our current volunteers (as identified above) to assess their experience in giving us their services. What do we do well? What needs improvement?

☐ We have polled the staff to learn what they already know about working with volunteers. Did they learn this on the job or through any formal training? What else do they feel they need to know?

☐ We have listened carefully to learn staff's *attitudes* and opinions about volunteers. Are they welcoming and enthusiastic at the idea of volunteer help, or resistant in any way? Are their opinions based on fact, personal experience, or misinformed stereotypes?

☐ We have made a special effort to survey and educate middle managers, unit supervisors, and others who will be important links in the chain to ensure that all staff are helped to work successfully with volunteers.

☐ We have assessed our physical environment and decided we have sufficient space, work surfaces, equipment (such as computers) and necessary tools, chairs and anything else needed to accommodate additional people: volunteers. Or we have identified potential space and resource issues and are budgeting to correct them.

☐ We have done some research as to how organizations in our community are recruiting and working with volunteers, and also how organizations similar to us do so. This information will help formulate our own plans.

☐ We have designated someone to be our "point person" for leading our volunteer involvement strategy, whether this is a new hire for the position of director of volunteer involvement or someone already on staff who has agreed to take on this responsibility as a part-time role while we get going. Either way, this person is skilled in volunteer management best practices.

☐ We have read *From the Top Down* and have used the tools here in *Leading the Way* so that we have thought through the executive-level decisions necessary to lay the foundation for volunteer involvement.

☐ We have designated an internal team of staff (including representation from the executive level) and volunteers to guide the creation or expansion of volunteer involvement within our organization.

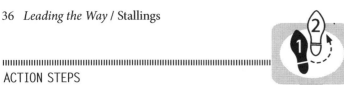

Planning a Volunteer Involvement Strategy

If you are establishing a volunteer initiative you should become familiar with the critical steps in preparing an organization to develop a strong foundation for volunteer involvement. All the steps need to be taken, but are not cleanly sequential; some overlap or need to be done simultaneously . Some can be carried out by one person or a combination of staff and volunteers. As applicable, we refer to other sections of the Toolkit (and elsewhere) where you can find materials to help you with each task.

Step 1

Think It Through

- Formulate your organization's philosophy of volunteer engagement (See Section 1.

- Carry out a needs assessment to determine organizational readiness to engage volunteers. (See Section 2.)

- Research and address risk management, insurance and legal issues in working with volunteers. (See Section 9. A great resource is www.nonprofitrisk.org.)

- Include volunteer involvement in the strategic planning of the organization. (See Section 2.)

Step 2

Designate Leadership and Allocate Resources

- Determine who will lead volunteer engagement and the best placement of that position within the organization. (See Section 4.)

- Determine appropriate resources needed to support volunteer engagement and create a corresponding budget to cover those needed resources. (See Section 3.)

(continued)

Planning a Volunteer Involvement Strategy
(continued)

Step 3:

Engage and Prepare the Entire Organization

- Determine expectations of staff who will partner with volunteers and include this responsibility in staff job and position descriptions. (See Section 6.)

- Design and conduct training for all staff and leadership volunteers who will partner with volunteers. (See Section 6.)

- Include staff and volunteers in the planning of volunteer involvement for their area of work.

Step 4:

Implement Best Practices in Engaging Volunteers—Ideally Initiated by the Director of Volunteer Involvement

- Create volunteer positions related to organizational priorities, staff needs, and client needs.

- In concert with upper management, develop essential guidelines, processes and policies related to volunteer engagement with the organization.

- Design appropriate screening techniques relative to volunteer positions.

- Develop orientation and training plans for volunteers.

- Select the best recordkeeping system to keep track of position descriptions, volunteers' histories of service to organization, recognition awarded, insurance updates, training records, etc.—and to generate necessary reports.

- Make certain that volunteer opportunities are prominent on the organization's Web site and in all organizational literature.

- Develop and implement a recruitment strategy.

- Prepare annual goals and objectives tied to the organization's strategic plan.

ACTION STEPS

Integrating Volunteer Engagement into Organizational Strategic Planning

A strategic plan is incomplete without consideration of how volunteers can help achieve the organization's mission and strategic goals. Executives and boards engaged in organizational planning should invite significant input from the person leading volunteer engagement within the organization. The following chart shares how the topic of volunteer engagement should be included in every aspect of organizational strategic planning.

Steps in Organizational Strategic Planning	How Volunteering Fits In
1. **Review the organization's vision and mission**	Discuss the role and value of volunteers. Ask, "Do we have a statement of philosophy of volunteer engagement and are we using it as a guide to involve volunteers in carrying out our mission?"
2. **Environmental scan:** What are the opportunities and challenges, both external and internal, most likely to affect the future of the organization?	Include information about trends in volunteering (such as desire for short-term volunteer commitment, availability of highly skilled volunteers), nationally and locally, and how these may affect our organization's involvement of volunteers. Introduce the opportunities and challenges of engaging new volunteers into the organization. Share how the characteristics of demographic and generational groups are changing the way people volunteer.
3. **Establish organizational goals,** being cognizant of challenges and opportunities found in the environmental scan	Discuss current or potential impact of volunteer engagement as it relates to specific organizational strategic goals. For each goal, ask how volunteers might be engaged to help reach the desired outcome.

Integrating Volunteer Engagement
into Organizational Strategic Planning

(continued)

Steps in Organizational Strategic Planning	How Volunteering Fits In
4. **Action planning:** What are the steps and time lines for reaching the established goals for the organization?	Depending on the action steps chosen, consider what enhancements/changes in volunteer involvement need to take place to achieve specific goals (e.g., recruiting more volunteers or volunteers with higher skill levels, better or new training of staff and/or volunteers, etc.) and time lines for achieving them. The person designated to lead volunteer involvement, along with key stakeholders, creates the operational plans for implementation.
5. **Budget** to carry out organizational goals/initiatives	Assess costs and resources associated with any change in volunteer involvement needed to carry out the established organizational goals and objectives. Adjust the budget accordingly.
6. **Appraise and evaluate** the organization's strategic plan	During any review/update phase of strategic planning, the leader of volunteer involvement reports progress, response, changes, impact of any action involving volunteers. Make adjustments as deemed appropriate.

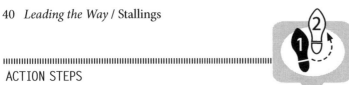

Align/Create Volunteer Positions in Response to Strategic Organizational Goals

As an executive, use these steps in collaboration with the director of volunteer involvement to design volunteer positions that align with the organization's strategic goals.

Step 1

State your organization's strategic goal:

Step 2

Ask: Are we currently engaging volunteers in any work related to this strategic goal?

- If no, why not?

- If yes, is it working? Should/could we do more?

Step 3

Design one or more volunteer position descriptions related to the strategic goal.

(continued)

Align/Create Volunteer Positions in Response to Strategic Organizational Goals

(continued)

Step 4

Determine what type(s) of volunteer(s) we might need to recruit to respond to this goal.

Step 5

Consider: How can these new volunteer positions potentially affect the strategic goal?

Step 6

Identify if support is available for staff to partner with these volunteers.

- If yes, what is that support?

- If no, what do we need to develop?

(continued)

Align/Create Volunteer Positions in Response to Strategic Organizational Goals
(continued)

Step 7

For each position needed, ask: What is the strategy for recruiting volunteers for this position?

- Are there potential internal candidates?

- Where will we take our message to find new volunteers to fill this position?

Step 8

Determine how to evaluate the success/impact of these positions and answer the questions below:

- How successfully did volunteers accomplish the intended impact?

- If they were not successful, why not?
  - ▷ Was our recruitment and/or placement faulty?
  - ▷ Do we need to modify the volunteer position to help reach the strategic goals?
  - ▷ Are there other causes?

A Starting Point
for Forming Policies Related to Volunteers

Adapted and updated from *Building Staff/Volunteer Relations* by
Ivan H. Scheier, ©2002, Energize, Inc.

There is wide agreement that articulating policies about volunteer involvement in an agency is highly desirable—but the policies need to be in writing, carefully considered, and regularly reconsidered. Policy statements should be reviewed and approved by the executive and/or board or generated by them.

Below are some subject areas that are suggested frequently as needing policy determination. The exact wording is, of course, up to each individual organization to consider. Note, too, that as policy, the statement does not intend to cover details of volunteer program implementation.

- A statement about the commitment to volunteer involvement in service delivery exists in the organization's mission statement.

- With every prospective new staff member, we explore and expect a positive, open-minded attitude about volunteers and related community resource development.

- Every staff job description includes a firm statement that volunteers are an important resource for accomplishing tasks and reaching goals.

- Every new staff member's orientation to the agency includes a thorough introduction to volunteer involvement.

- In-service training for staff includes developing the specific skills necessary for supervising and working with volunteers effectively.

- All staff are expected to develop meaningful assignments for volunteers.

- There are definite incentives or rewards for staff who work well with volunteers.

- "How are you involving the community in your work?" is the kind of question asked of each staff member during his or her performance evaluation.

- Each top management person shall model the agency's commitment to volunteers by recruiting and supervising at least one volunteer.

- Affirmative action policy and values apply equally to engaging volunteers.

(continued)

A Starting Point
for Forming Policies Related to Volunteers
(continued)

- Volunteers will be held to the same confidentiality and privacy standards as paid staff.

- Volunteers are held to performance standards, are evaluated on a periodic basis, and can be reassigned or terminated for poor performance.

- We conduct a risk management assessment of volunteer activities and create a safe environment for everyone. Also, we do not allow fear of risk to limit what the right volunteer can do.

- Volunteers will be given the tools and resources they need to do their assignments effectively, including access to the organization's intranet and other online materials.

- We consider volunteer involvement real work and will provide references for paid employment and college applications, etc. for volunteers on that basis.

- Volunteer work in the agency does not in any way preclude a person's full consideration for paid employment in our agency. On the other hand, it does not guarantee such employment.

- Clear and effective grievance procedures will be open to both volunteers and staff on matters that may need to be resolved between them, or between either and the agency.

- Wherever possible, volunteers shall be treated as staff.

- Wherever possible, staff shall be treated with all the consideration given to volunteers.

Volunteer Policies and Procedures

Policies and procedures must be developed by each organization as relevant to its specific setting and situation. There is no one-size-fits-all language. To demonstrate this, see the two real-life examples below of policies and procedures related to selecting/screening volunteers. The first example meets the needs of a local library, but the second example is far more detailed and complex because the Court Appointed Special Advocates (CASA) program has to meet legal requirements and national standards.

Greenfield Public Library
Greenfield
MA

Selection of Volunteers

Volunteers are selected based on their qualifications in relation to the needs of the library at any given time, and based on their ability to commit to a consistent schedule of volunteer hours. Selection of in-house volunteers is the responsibility of the Director and/or Asst. Director in conjunction with the Volunteer Coordinator; selection of delivery volunteers is the responsibility of the Homebound Volunteer Coordinator.

Prospective volunteers are requested to fill out an application form and will be interviewed by one of the above individuals. If there are no suitable volunteer opportunities, application forms will be kept on file for a period of one year. Applicants will be called if a project is identified which matches their interests or qualifications.

http://greenfieldpubliclibrary.org/Volunteer.html

CASA of Allegheny County
PA

d. Volunteer Screening Policies

To ensure that volunteers accepted into the CASA program are competent and of good character, CASA of Allegheny County carefully screens all volunteer applicants using the following procedures:

(1) *The applicant must submit a written application containing information concerning personal experiences with child abuse and/or neglect, educational background, employment, volunteer history and experience working with children.*

(2) *The applicant shall participate in a personal interview with a CASA staff member.*

(3) *The applicant must provide three (3) references from persons unrelated to the applicant, at least two (2) of whom have directly supervised the applicant.*

(4) *The CASA program will conduct a formal security check of the volunteer applicant by screening criminal records through the Pennsylvania State Police and the Central Child Abuse Registry.*

If the applicant has lived in another state within the last five (5) years, the CASA program will conduct a formal criminal records background check with that state…[section continues as part of a ten-page document]

http://nc.casaforchildren.org/files/public/community/programs/IndicatorsCompliance/0804_volunteer_policies_and_procedures_0053.pdf

(continued)

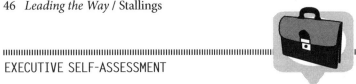

EXECUTIVE SELF-ASSESSMENT

Do I plan for volunteer involvement and develop appropriate policies with these actions?

1. I lead discussions regarding our desires for initiating (or re-designing) our volunteer involvement strategy.

    ☐ Yes   ☐ No   ☐ Sometimes   ☐ Will now initiate   ☐ Not relevant

2. I conduct needs assessments or review the results of these assessments to gather significant information to design or redesign volunteer engagement within our organization.

    ☐ Yes   ☐ No   ☐ Sometimes   ☐ Will now initiate   ☐ Not relevant

3. I am aware of the major steps for initiating volunteer involvement and have led or supported these planning/action steps.

    ☐ Yes   ☐ No   ☐ Sometimes   ☐ Will now initiate   ☐ Not relevant

4. I encourage all functions, programs, and units of the organization (including volunteer services) to annually design priorities/goals for the upcoming year with action plans to achieve them.

    ☐ Yes   ☐ No   ☐ Sometimes   ☐ Will now initiate   ☐ Not relevant

5. I support involvement of the leader of volunteer resources in strategic planning for the organization.

    ☐ Yes   ☐ No   ☐ Sometimes   ☐ Will now initiate   ☐ Not relevant

6. I invite the input of volunteers themselves at appropriate phases of our strategic planning.

    ☐ Yes   ☐ No   ☐ Sometimes   ☐ Will now initiate   ☐ Not relevant

7. As I expect of all staff, I design positions for volunteers to report to me that are in alignment with our strategic priorities/goals.

    ☐ Yes   ☐ No   ☐ Sometimes   ☐ Will now initiate   ☐ Not relevant

8. Working with my board of directors and senior management, I lead or monitor efforts to create policies and procedures that will ensure the most effective volunteer involvement in our organization.

    ☐ Yes   ☐ No   ☐ Sometimes   ☐ Will now initiate   ☐ Not relevant

Budgeting for and Funding Volunteer Involvement

The most significant thing that I do to contribute to the effectiveness of the volunteer program is to highlight its importance to our funders. I tell business leaders that we are a community of volunteers, young and old, and that it's people's voluntary activities that are going to successfully transform problems such as the achievement gap and under-development among poor youth. I tell them we need money for supporting and cultivating this kind of volunteerism and community building.

Gabrielle L. Kurlander, President
All Stars Project, Inc.
New York, New York

I am always surprised by how many agencies keep their volunteer database and their donor base separate. Sometimes the volunteer director and the development director don't even speak to each other. Yet, they are both working with people who support the cause, with time and/or money, and who may be willing to give more if they're simply asked.

Wanda Bailey, former Executive Director
Volunteer San Diego
San Diego, California

CONTENTS

CONCEPTS IN DEPTH The tools in this section apply the concepts discussed at length in the book, *From the Top Down: The Executive Role in Successful Volunteer Involvement, 3rd edition*, by Susan J. Ellis (Philadelphia: Energize, Inc., 2010), specifically:

- Chapter 1: Why Volunteers? – Section on "The Volunteer-Donor Connection"
- Chapter 3: Budgeting, Allocating, and Finding Resources
- Chapter 11: The Financial Value of Volunteer Contributions

Introduction to the Executive Role

I n my 2005 study of CEO volunteer champions, executives perceived lack of funding for volunteer engagement as the number one challenge to success. Although some misinterpret volunteer time as a completely free resource, most of us know that effective volunteer involvement requires funds for, at a minimum, leadership staff and office supplies. Research demonstrates that building the organization's capacity to engage volunteers successfully has extensive and positive impact on extending the organization's ability to carry out its mission through service, advocacy, and the generation of resources. Therefore, finding the necessary funding is worth the effort.

Also, as executives recognize the close connection between satisfied volunteers and corresponding financial contributions to the organization, attention is turning to the subject of raising funds specifically to support volunteer engagement efforts. But to seek funding, executives must anticipate and identify what resources are necessary to support volunteer engagement effectively. They need to develop a realistic budget reflecting projected expenses and other needs, such as workspace and staff time.

Raising funds specifically for volunteer involvement can be done once a strong case is built for how the costs of volunteer involvement can be leveraged into many more multiples of vital services. Success in raising funds requires the executive to strengthen collaboration among top-level management, development staff, and staff managing volunteers. (In section seven, we will explore this collaboration in more depth.)

Often, volunteers raise significant funds for an organization but rarely, if ever, are any of these volunteer-generated funds directly allocated to support the expenses related to volunteer engagement. It is time to explore this option. Without executive leadership supporting the concept, it will have little chance of being initiated.

This section presents ideas for building the case for donors to support volunteer involvement financially and addresses some of the obstacles to financial support of volunteer involvement. It also expands thinking about ways to invite volunteers to become financial donors themselves as well as reach out to their sphere of contacts to generate resources for the organization.

> *"Raising funds specifically for volunteer involvement can be done once a strong case is built for how the costs of volunteer involvement can be leveraged into many more... vital services."*

Budgeting for Volunteer Involvement

Chapter three in From the Top Down *(Ellis 2010) deals in depth with the categories of expenses required to support volunteer engagement. This worksheet provides space to consider each possible expense category described there.*

PERSONNEL

Director of Volunteer Involvement
(Full-time or _____ hours per week) $ _____

Assistant Director of Volunteer Involvement
(Full-time or _____ hours per week)   _____

Secretary/Administrative Assistant   _____

Other assigned staff: _____   _____

(While not a direct expense, the cost of staff time to train and supervise volunteers at the work-unit level is one of the indirect expenses to be considered.)

Benefits (estimated @ _____% of total salaries)   _____

                                Subtotal: Personnel: $_____

OPERATIONAL COSTS

Note that initial start-up costs are differentiated by an "S." Most of these items are one-time expenditures, though several also involve additional purchases each year as volunteer involvement grows or inventory needs to be replenished.

Furniture and Equipment:

Office furniture for the volunteer office,
including desks, chairs, lamps, etc. $ _____ S

File cabinets   _____ S

Computer(s)/typewriter(s)   _____ S

Coat racks, storage cabinets, lounge
furniture, etc. for volunteers   _____ S

Bulletin boards and exhibit equipment   _____ S

Slide projector and screen   _____ S

(continued)

Budgeting for Volunteer Involvement
(continued)

Other equipment:

_____   _____   S

_____   _____   S

_____   _____

Subtotal: Furn/Equip: $_____

Software and Internet Technology:

Volunteer management recordkeeping software $_____   S

E-mail management software   _____   S

Web-based services   _____

Other technology   _____

Subtotal: Technology: $_____

Telephone:

Installation of instruments $_____   S

Monthly service charge x 12   _____

Toll calls/long distance x 12   _____

Reimbursement to volunteers for calls
made on agency's behalf   _____

Subtotal: Telephone: $_____

Supplies:

Office and maintenance supplies
estimated @ ($____ per person per year)
x (number of employees + FTE volunteer staff) $_____

Other supplies or tools needed
by volunteers to do their work properly:

_____   _____

_____   _____

_____   _____   *(continued)*

Budgeting for Volunteer Involvement
(continued)

Purchase of uniforms, smocks, vests or any
clothing required to be worn when volunteering _____

Subtotal: Supplies: $_____

Publishing, Printing, and Reproduction:

Photocopying ($____/mo. x 12) $_____

Printing of volunteer office forms   _____ S

Design and printing of recruitment materials
(both initial and ongoing expense;
some quality pieces plus numerous
photocopied flyers)   _____

Printing of recognition certificates,
periodic volunteer newsletter, etc.   _____

Printing of volunteer program
manual/handbook   _____ S

Other:

_____   _____

_____   _____

_____   _____

*Note need to reprint inventory of some of the
above as an ongoing expense.*

Subtotal: Printing: $_____

Postage:

Regular correspondence, $____/mo. x 12 $_____

Periodic mass mailings for recruitment,
bulk mailing of newsletter, etc.   _____

Subtotal: Postage: $_____

(continued)

Budgeting for Volunteer Involvement
(continued)

Insurance:

(May be included in overall agency policy,
or a special rider, or a specific new policy.)

Subtotal: Insurance: $_____

Recognition:

(Depending on event, may include food costs,
entertainment, hall rental, gifts, pins, etc.)

Subtotal: Recognition: $_____

Enabling Funds:

Reimbursement for volunteer mileage
or transportation $_____

Reimbursement to volunteers for
out-of-pocket expenses incurred
while serving clients (e.g., purchase of
art supplies, taking a child to the zoo, etc.)   _____

Purchase or loan of volunteer uniforms
or special clothing   _____

Other reimbursements:

_____   _____

_____   _____

_____   _____

Subtotal: Enabling Funds: $_____

Travel:

Volunteer office staff local and intermediate
distance travel for recruitment outreach $_____

Travel to state or national conferences
(for volunteer program staff and
designated volunteers)   _____

Subtotal: Travel: $_____

(continued)

Budgeting for Volunteer Involvement
(continued)

Professional Development:

Registration fees for seminars,
conferences, etc. (for volunteer office
staff and designated volunteers) $ _____

Journal subscriptions, books, etc.   _____

Membership fees for professional associations   _____

Subtotal: Prof. Dev.: $_____

Volunteer Training:

Reproduction of handout materials
or purchase of books for volunteers $ _____

Slides and other training materials   _____

Film/video rental or purchase fees   _____

Speaker fees   _____

Subtotal: Training: $_____

Other:

_____ $ _____

_____   _____

_____   _____

Subtotal: Other: $_____

TOTAL COSTS: $_____

Other Resource Allocation

The following items which support volunteers may already be available in your organization. Even though these may not require a new line item in the budget, you may want to "charge" them to the volunteer office or need to raise the amount of money allocated to them to accommodate increased use by volunteers.

Staff time

☐ Time required to orient, train, and support volunteers by front line staff members designated as their supervisors or liaisons

☐ Collaboration from departments or staff whose special expertise is needed by the volunteer program, such as marketing, Internet technology, budget/finance, fund development, etc.

Space

☐ Adequate work space for the volunteer program staff and volunteers

☐ Private interviewing area

☐ Locked area for volunteers to leave personal belongings

☐ Training and meeting rooms

☐ Other:

_____

_____

Maintenance services

☐ Setting up rooms for volunteer training/orientation/events

☐ Cleaning of area used by volunteers
☐ Other:

_____

_____

Volunteer benefits

Items on this list may or may not be applicable, based on the positions volunteers fill, the amount of time they spend on site, and the facility itself (i.e., whether safety goggles must be worn or if there is a cafeteria).

☐ Coffee, tea and snacks

☐ Meals on days worked

☐ Parking privileges

☐ Free admission to facility events/performances

☐ Discounts in facility store

☐ Free learning opportunities/training

☐ Other:

_____

_____

Challenges in Raising Funds to Support Volunteer Involvement

> Many issues impinge on an organization's ability to raise adequate funds to support volunteer engagement. Anticipate possible roadblocks, and brainstorm how you might overcome these challenges.

- Lack of resources for volunteer involvement can often be linked to an executive not truly committed to allocating or generating funds for this effort. While touted as the "heart of the organization," in practice, volunteers are not a priority to be supported with adequate resources. So, ask yourself:

  - Do we demonstrate how much we value volunteers by covering the costs of their involvement appropriately?

  - Is there really no money to pay the costs of involving volunteers or are they simply too a low priority to receive funds?

  - Have we attempted to find funding for volunteers or ever submitted a proposal to obtain funds?

  - Do we routinely include a line item to cover volunteer-related expenses in every funding proposal we develop, if volunteers will be involved in delivering the proposed service?

- The term volunteer can cause tremendous problems in fundraising. For many people the word means "free help" and thus compromises requests for resources, both internally and externally.

- Currently corporations and other funders and leaders in the field are preferring to use terms such as pro bono service, citizen or civic engagement, human capital, and other terms to refer to those donating time to organizations. When requesting funds to support this activity, use the terms most relevant to the funder.

- Staff resistance to volunteers can derail attempts to secure resources for supporting volunteer involvement. Apart from other causes of such resistance, employees may be concerned that increasing funds to recruit more volunteers might lead to reducing the number of paid staff.

(continued)

Challenges in Raising Funds
to Support Volunteer Involvement
(continued)

- Often, raising money to support successful volunteer engagement is no one's responsibility. Directors of volunteer involvement do not have this task in their job descriptions, while development staff cannot articulate the case or rationale for supporting volunteers to potential funders.

- If volunteer engagement is always described as a program of the organization, it can be perceived as being in competition with other programs serving the clients of the organization, thus dropping to the bottom of anyone's to-do list. No one would say that the human resources office runs an "employee program"; both paid staff and volunteers work to deliver program services.

- Historically, most funders have not looked at how organizations involve citizens in their work, with the possible exception of the make-up and capability of their boards of directors. There is a movement to counter this, but it will take a lot of education to equip funders with the knowledge and tools to see the significance of evaluating organizations on their full engagement of the community.

- Development staff and volunteer management staff need to work together to develop resources and collaborative, not competitive, outreach strategies. A "silo mentality" creates a false dichotomy—and sometimes duplication of efforts—in approaching prospective money donors and recruiting volunteers, who are time donors.

- Executives rarely pay attention to the correlation between donors and volunteers. Both types of supporters are significant to the "resource mix," yet both executives and funders know they must pay for fundraising. The same logic should extend to volunteer "friend raising." Ask yourself:

  - How many volunteers give money as well as time?

  - Are financial donors also invited to give time and skills?

  - Is there a continuum or life cycle of involvement in which people move in and out of both methods of support to the organization?

Key Questions to Think through before Contacting Potential Funders

1. What problem or need is your organization addressing?

   _____

   _____

2. Who or what is affected by the problem?

   _____

   _____

3. How will volunteer involvement help to address the problem?

   _____

   _____

4. What are some specific benefits of engaging volunteers in this program/initiative/organization (time and other resources contributed by volunteers, the community learns about your mission via word of mouth, more people can be served, etc.)?

   _____

   _____

5. How is your organization unique in addressing the problem?

   _____

   _____

6. What is the anticipated or desired outcome of the effort?

   _____

   _____

7. What will it cost to reach the desired outcome? (Budget for both cash expenses and donated resources, whether people, funds, or in-kind services.)

   _____

   _____

(continued)

Key Questions to Think through
before Contacting Potential Funders
(continued)

8. Which donor(s) or funder(s) will we ask for support and why?

_____

_____

   a. Who shares our interest in having an impact on this need/problem?

_____

_____

   b. How will each prospective donor or funder benefit from giving us support?

_____

_____

Where to Research Potential Funding for Volunteer Involvement

In the United States (with some access from other countries)

1. **The Foundation Center**
   http://www.foundationcenter.org

   Supported by close to 550 foundations, the Foundation Center is recognized as the nation's leading authority on organized philanthropy and maintains the most comprehensive database on U.S. grantmakers and their grants. Their resources can be accessed through the Center's Web site, five regional library/learning centers, and a national network of more than 425 Cooperating Collections at libraries, nonprofit resource centers, and organizations in every U.S. state and Puerto Rico and in Australia, Brazil, Mexico, Nigeria, South Korea, and Thailand. The Center's online subscription database, *Foundation Directory Online*, provides detailed information about more than 98,000 U.S. foundations and corporate donors and 1.7 million grants. It can be used free of charge on site at all Center locations and Cooperating Collections. You can search by key interest areas, including volunteer involvement and related phrases.

2. **Programs under the Serve America Act**
   http://www.nationalservice.gov/for_organizations/funding/index.asp

   In 2009, the Edward M. Kennedy Serve America Act established three new programs designed to channel money and/or services to nonprofit organizations, specifically to increase capacity in community and volunteer engagement: Nonprofit Capacity Building Program (NCBP); Social Innovation Fund (SIF); and the Volunteer Generation Fund (VGF). These funds are administered by the Corporation for National and Community Service and must be re-appropriated by Congress each year.

3. **Grantmakers for Effective Organizations (GEO)**
   http://www.geofunders.org

   Three hundred fifty grant-making organizations who have expressed interest in funding organizations to improve their organizational effectiveness. This organization was founded by James Irvine, Ewing Marion Kauffman and David and Lucile Packard Foundations in 1997. All of their members are listed at: http://wwwgeofunders.org/currentmembers.aspx.

(continued)

Where to Research Potential Funding
for Volunteer Involvement
(continued)

Idea: An excellent volunteer task would be to review the interests of these grantmakers to determine any potential matches with your mission and your needs to build capacity to carry out that mission. Building a stronger volunteer base is certainly a significant way to build capacity.

4. **PACE – Philanthropy for Active Civic Engagement**
http://www.pacefunders.org

PACE is "a learning community of grantmakers and donors" with the mission to inspire interest, understanding and investment in civic engagement. Seventeen major foundations are involved, including the Case Foundation, Craigslist Foundation, Bill and Melinda Gates Foundation, W.K. Kellogg Foundation, The Ms. Foundation for Women.

5. **HEP Development**
http://www.hepdevelopment.com

This organization keeps up to date with all corporations/businesses that give matching funds. They claim that 1 in 10 gifts could be matched. It is a fee-based service. Letting donors and volunteers know names of businesses in your area that match donated funds can significantly increase the total amount you raise.

6. **Dollars for Doers**

Many corporations/businesses have a program to give a financial donation to nonprofit organizations where their employees volunteer. This matching gift concept is most often—but not always—called "Dollars for Doers," but there is no centralized organization nor any standardization. This means there is no list of companies with such programs. Use your favorite Internet search engine and type in the phrase "Dollars for Doers" to see what might be operating in your community. Alternately, search the Web sites of local companies to see if they offer this type of donation.

7. *Resource Guide on Volunteer Management Funding* (2010)
http://www.reimaginingservice.org/ResourceGuide.aspx

Produced by the Reimagining Service Funding Action Team to: 1) help nonprofits make the case for funding to support volunteer management and 2) to share information with funders on the value and need for providing this type

(continued)

Where to Research Potential Funding for Volunteer Involvement
(continued)

of financial support. It includes tools for calculating return-on-investment, research on the connection between volunteer management and agency capacity, successful proposals to various funding sources, a best practices section with articles on how to seek funding for volunteer management, and more. Online and free, Reimagining Service intends to expand and update this Guide as time goes on.

Outside of the United States

1. **Multi-country search sites:**

   - Michigan State University Libraries maintains a comprehensive list and links for **"International and Foreign Grant Makers"** at http://staff.lib.msu.edu/harris23/grants/privint.htm

   - **European Foundation Centre**
     http://www.efc.be/

   - **Asia Pacific Philanthropy Information Network**
     http://www.asiapacificphilanthropy.org
     Includes information about philanthropy and the third sector in Australia, China, Hong Kong SAR, Japan, Philippines, Republic of Korea, Taiwan, and Thailand. Includes information about funding activities as well.

2. **Canada**

   - **Canadian Grant-Giving Foundations**
     http://www.charityvillage.com/cv/nonpr/nonpr17.asp
     List compiled by CharityVillage.com. Also see http://www.charityvillage.com/cv/guides/guide8.asp

3. **United Kingdom**

   - **Awards for All**
     http://www.awardsforall.org.uk/
     This is a local grants initiative of The Big Lottery Fund, http://www.big-lotteryfund.org.uk/

   - **The Baring Foundation**
     http://www.baringfoundation.org.uk/

(continued)

Where to Research Potential Funding
for Volunteer Involvement
(continued)

- **Department of Health Volunteering Fund for Health and Social Care**
  http://www.volunteeringfund.com/index.htm

- **Red Foundation**
  http://www.redfoundation.org/

- **The Volunteer Centre Edinburgh**
  Maintains a page on "Funding Volunteering"
  http://www.volunteeredinburgh.org.uk/resources/funding.htm

4. **Australia:**

   - **A Guide to Community Grants (Australia)**
     http://www.aph.gov.au/library/intguide/sp/spgrants.htm

   - **Volunteer Grants from the Department of Families, Housing, Community Services and Indigenous Affairs (FaHCSIA)**
     http://www.fahcsia.gov.au/sa/volunteers/progserv/pages/volunteergrants.aspx

KEY CONCEPT

Constructing a Case Statement for Donors to Support Volunteer Engagement

There are two essential rules when constructing a case statement to make financial support of volunteer involvement credible.

1. **DON'T approach funders with a budget to support the infrastructure of running a volunteer program.**

    - Infrastructure supports your organization, not your clients. Focusing on internal needs is the biggest mistake in fundraising!

    - Speaking of a "volunteer program" isolates community participation into a special project, possibly viewed in competition with more client-centered "programs." Remember, you would not refer to an "employee program," would you?

      An Ineffective Ask:
      We need money to fund the position of a volunteer coordinator so that the program runs more smoothly and efficiently and our volunteers have a more organized and successful experience.

      Probable Funder Response:
      How are you different than any other organization that would like a volunteer coordinator? What difference would it make in carrying out your mission?

2. **DO** request funding that **will empower volunteers to expand the reach of your mission.**

    - Whatever your mission—ending hunger, improving the environment, enabling seniors to live independently—it is that goal with which funders will want to be identified and which they will likely support.

      An Effective Ask:
      Divorce, alcoholism, drug abuse, and depression are frequently associated with those who must care for seriously ill children. We are looking for funds to extend our support to approximately 1,300 families in our region who care for a child with a serious illness. Expanding the number of community volunteers (more targeted recruitment) and strengthening their skills (formal training) to provide respite services will allow us to increase and enhance our overall service to these families.

      Probable Funder Response:
      We share your interest in extending assistance to additional families with a seriously ill child and will consider your request of maximizing the support through service provided by an increased number of effectively trained volunteers.

Preparing to Respond to
Possible Donor Objections

You may need to educate a prospective funder about the value of volunteers and their abilities. Therefore, before you make your funding request, consider all the objections, or at least concerns, a donor or funder might have when deciding whether to give you money. Then, prepare your responses. Here is an example:

Donor Objection: "My experience is that volunteers are not reliable and you might find yourself investing more in them than they return in service to the organization."

Potential Response: "I am sorry that you have had that experience with volunteers. In our organization, we do a very thorough job of selecting the right volunteers for positions available, hold volunteers accountable, and treat them as partners in our important mission. We have had remarkable success with volunteers carrying out the commitment they pledge to us. We hold re-commitment discussions with volunteers every quarter so that we can detect any dissatisfaction or needs for additional training or a change in position."

What are the potential objections you anticipate hearing in response to your request for funds to support your involvement of volunteers? How will you respond?

Possible Donor Objection	Your Potential Response

KEY CONCEPT

Talking Points to Gain Donor Support for Volunteer Involvement

"We are leveraging resources when engaging volunteers."

A buzzword for funders is *leveraging*. They want their gift to have the greatest effect and therefore be multiplied, both in cash value and in more services or impact (more bang for the buck). Think of all the ways that supporting volunteers in your organization will provide leveraging opportunities:

- Donated time by many people will attract other resources, including matched gifts and word-of-mouth publicity

- Expanded services (for example, volunteers can provide services during hours when many employees might not work)

- Successful innovative ideas shared with others providing a similar service. Offer to write up your findings and share with those who could adapt your techniques.

"All funded programs need community oversight."

Any organization that receives private donations or public support is truly owned by the community. Therefore, engaging volunteers from the community in the effort makes a great deal of sense, both as watchdogs for use of the money and as individuals who can expand the services.

"Volunteers extend our services beyond what our budget could buy."

Always avoid saying "volunteers *save* us money." In most cases, volunteers are not actually saving the organization money as the organization could not have spent funds they didn't have. The reality is that volunteers *expand the budget* and *extend the services* of the organization. If we perpetuate the thought that volunteers save organizations money, we are also implying that, if we had all the funds we needed, volunteers would be expendable. This is not true because volunteers are more valuable than the costs involved in supporting them.

(continued)

Talking Points to Gain Donor Support
for Volunteer Involvement
(continued)

"The return on investment (ROI) with volunteers is tremendous when they are strategically deployed and well managed."

Be confident that the investment of dollars and time to the support volunteers provides a significant return to the organization. ROI is increasingly of great interest to private and public funders. While it is difficult to put an exact value on the time a volunteer mentors a child or advocates for a clean environment, we can still speak in terms of the outcomes and impact of the work of volunteers. For example:

- *Last year, our volunteer tutors prepared twenty-five low-income, high-risk young people for successful entrance into a junior college.*

- *With the organized support of regular volunteer visits, we have successfully helped fifty seniors over age eighty-five to stay in their homes independently for a longer period of time than they could before.*

- *A team of pro bono volunteers skilled in software development upgraded our existing software and developed new report formats so that we now can track client service benchmarks clearly.*

"Studies have shown that organizations with a designated, full-time director of volunteer resources are far more effective in involving volunteers as partners in furthering their mission."

Here are two excerpts of research reports connecting the impact of employing volunteer management staff to more effective volunteer involvement. A complete listing of studies on this topic can be found in the second edition of *Volunteer Management: Mobilizing All the Resources of the Community*, Chapter 16, "Enhancing the Status of the Volunteer Program" (McCurley and Lynch 2010).

1. Grantmaker Forum on Community and National Service, *The Cost of a Volunteer*, March 2003 http://www.pacefunders.org/archivesw.html

   In order to accommodate more volunteers, program managers say they need more organizational capacity—more professional staff, more funding, more infrastructure. Of the nine programs that stated they do in fact need

(continued)

Talking Points to Gain Donor Support
for Volunteer Involvement

(continued)

more volunteers, their needs are specific in terms of scheduling and skills. The key issue is having the capacity to incorporate volunteer labor effectively so that neither the organization nor the volunteer is wasting time.

2. Urban Institute, *Volunteer Management Capacity in America's Charities and Congregations,* February 2004 http://www.urban.org/UploadedPDF/410963_VolunteerManagment.pdf

The percentage of time a paid staff volunteer coordinator devotes to volunteer management is positively related to the capacity of organizations to take on additional volunteers. The best prepared and most effective volunteer programs are those with paid staff members who dedicate a substantial portion of their time to management of volunteers. This study demonstrated that, as staff time spent on volunteer management increased, adoption of volunteer management practices increased as well. Moreover, investments in volunteer management and benefits derived from volunteers feed on each other, with investments bringing benefits and these benefits justify greater investments.

"Volunteers are often financial donors, too."

Increasingly, financial contributors practice a blend of philanthropy and service in their nonprofit investments. One finding in a 2009 study by Fidelity® Charitable Gift Fund and VolunteerMatch (http://www.charitablegift.org/learn-about-charity/news/12-03-2009.shtml) was that "volunteers donate, on average, ten times more money than non-volunteers." Therefore, the number of volunteers committed to your organization can tremendously affect the financial bottom line of the organization.

What is the aggregate annual financial gift of current and past volunteers in your organization? It may surprise you!

Methods for Raising Funds
for Volunteer Involvement

Methods	Using	Not using	N/A	Will explore
1. Seek donations from *current* volunteers.				
2. Seek donations from former volunteers.				
3. Outreach to corporations/businesses.				
4. Research local companies with matching gift programs or "Dollars for Doers" programs. Then share that information with volunteers and other potential donors.				
5. Submit proposals to foundations with interest in your mission or in citizen involvement.				
6. Hold fundraising events (specifically to support volunteer involvement). Engage volunteers to help plan, attend, sponsor, donate products, invite friends/business colleagues, etc.				
7. Spread the word that you accept "Gifts in Honor of Volunteers" for commemorative or special occasions, or in memory of volunteers.				
8. Ask volunteers (and others) for donations of in-kind goods to be used by volunteers.				
9. Tell volunteers and other potential donors that they can designate a percentage of the financial resources listed below to be earmarked for the support of volunteer engagement: • Appreciated property/life insurance • Charitable gift annuities • Charitable remainder trusts • Bequests and naming opportunities • Endowments, memorial and commemorative gifts • Securities and real estate				
10. Offer methods of designating all or part of a donation to support volunteer involvement on all donation requests in print and online. Allow sponsorships or other revenue to be similarly earmarked to support volunteers.				

Three Questions about Connecting Time and Money Donors

1. Should we ask volunteers to give money as well as time?

YES, because…

- Volunteers are closest to the work of the organization and are therefore likely to have a stronger commitment to your mission than those not involved in your work.

- Volunteers are in the best position to understand that you need money as well as their time. They see what paid staff do and what items you need for clients.

- Done with sensitivity and appreciation that they already give the valuable gift of their time, the invitation to donate financially gives volunteers the opportunity they deserve to be full contributors.

- Studies show that volunteers give far more than non-volunteers. Generally the higher the commitment and involvement, the larger the gift will be.

Other Things to Consider When Inviting Volunteers to Contribute Financially

- Involve volunteers in thinking through the best ways to invite them to give financially.

- Your organization should keep track of all financial and in-kind resources that come through the efforts of volunteers. That figure should be added to the value that volunteers contribute to the organization.

- Suggest that some of the money raised through volunteer efforts be designated to support volunteer involvement.

- When designing a program to promote gifts given in honor of volunteers on their birthdays or special occasions, be sure to develop a system for recording such gifts.

- If volunteers are associated with any companies having matching gift or Dollars for Doers programs, make sure they know that their time and gifts can be leveraged for even greater impact.

(continued)

Three Questions about Connecting
Time and Money Donors
(continued)

- Keep volunteers abreast of needs in the organization (both physical, such as computers, and personnel, such as skills in photography). From volunteers' social circles can come many sources of additional support to the organization.

- Ask volunteers to consider donating unused miles or hotel points. The organization can use them as raffle prizes or for use when one of their staff/volunteers wants to attend a conference.

- Volunteers often ask that the money spent on lavish recognition be diminished and the money be used to serve the clients/cause of the organization. Offer volunteers an opportunity to cover the costs of meals, etc., at recognition events if you hear this concern.

- A letter asking for a financial donation from a volunteer should be a personal invitation acknowledging his or her service to the organization, not a standardized letter sent to all potential donors.

- Make sure that former volunteers who have left in good standing are also given a special letter asking for support—not the one-letter-fits-all approach!

2. Should we ask financial donors to give time as well as money?

YES, because...

- Funds do not magically appear; we should value the person as much as the bank account. Offering the opportunity to volunteer as well as to give money is always positive (even if the donor chooses not to give time) because it implies "we think you can be of help."

- After years of giving, donor fatigue can set in and people wonder if they should continue giving to the same cause. It has been shown that, when asked to volunteer skills and talents as well as give money, donors tend to recommit to the cause—again, even if they do not actually volunteer.

(continued)

Three Questions about Connecting
Time and Money Donors
(continued)

- The person writing the check is not necessarily the only one in that family interested in your cause. Adding a message about volunteer opportunities to a funding appeal may therefore uncover spouses, adult children, and friends who want to get involved.

- Always remember that your volunteers and financial donors may already be the same people! So be sure to check your records first.

3. How should we request/respond to financial gifts from donors who are also volunteers?

- Ask current donors of time and money if they would be willing to write personal notes on letters that will go to people who only donate or volunteer and who might be intrigued to contribute in new ways.

- Think of a special way to recognize donors of both time and money during any recognition event as a way to encourage some donors to become volunteers and vice versa.

- Introduce the idea of having volunteers designate their gift to be given totally or partially in support of the resources it takes to involve them as volunteers.

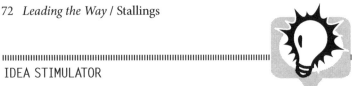

Inviting Volunteers to Consider
a First-Time Financial Contribution

A generic donation request letter could offend a volunteer by communicating that you haven't noticed his or her hard work. The template below has ideas for crafting a letter showing appreciation as well as asking the volunteer to support the organization even further.

Salutation:

Dear *[insert name]*,

Open with recognition:
Specify what the individual does as a volunteer. Personalize even more by indicating which clients benefited and any specific recent events in which the volunteer participated.

We are so grateful to you for your service as a volunteer *[describe what they do]* in our organization. Your generous contribution of time *[is/was]* valued by our organization and especially our clients who *[are/were]* the ultimate beneficiaries of your service.

Acknowledge a connection:
Use language that relates to your mission such as "build a more environmentally conscious world."

As someone who *[is/has been]* close to our mission, you are the most aware of our ever-increasing needs to garner resources, both personnel and financial, to better serve our clients.

Make the ask:
Present the invitation to support the mission with funds as well as time by indicating a specific goal or initiative.

If you feel that you are able and willing to make a financial contribution toward *[a specific goal or project]* we would be delighted to receive it.

Assure that volunteering is still valued even without a financial donation:

We want to offer you this annual opportunity, but we also want you to know that if you are unable or choose not to contribute in this manner, we are, and always will be, grateful for your precious gift of time, your skills, and your dedication to *[our mission]*. This letter comes to you, not with any pressure or obligation, but with an opportunity to share your financial resources, if you are able and so inclined.

Repeat thanks:

Thank you, again, for your faithful service to *[our mission]*.

(continued)

Inviting Volunteers to Consider
a First-Time Financial Contribution
(continued)

Signature:
Should be the executive director, a board member, or a current volunteer who also gives and is willing to be the chair of outreach to other volunteers.

Sincerely,
Name
Title
Your Organization

Postscript *(Optional):*
Provide a way for the volunteer to request not to be contacted about donating—be sure to include specific instructions how to do this.

P.S. If you would prefer not to be invited to contribute in the future, simply let us know and your name will be removed from the list until such time as you indicate to us that you would like to receive such an invitation.

► **Personal Note:** *If possible, a brief handwritten personal note by the person sending the letter or some other appropriate person can make a big difference.*

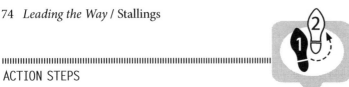

Gifts in Honor of Volunteers

Many people feel uncomfortable about getting presents from family and friends on their birthday or other special occasions, preferring instead to request that a financial donation be made to a charitable cause important to them. Why not suggest a gift in honor of their volunteer work with your organization? Here's how:

Step 1

Form a task force, with volunteer representatives, to design the gifts-in-honor program and the materials to support it.

Step 2

Let the task force create cards and forms for volunteers to give to their friends and family to explain the gift option. The cards can be serious or humorous. Also offer the option of gifts-in-honor on your Web site. The descriptive card can give prospective donors the opportunity to send in a donation or go to the Web site.

Sample Card: Request for Gifts in Honor of a Volunteer

Dear (first name)

On my [special occasion, anniversary, birthday], *please consider giving a gift to the organization where I volunteer:* [Homeless Shelter Haven]. *I am a great supporter of their work and hope you will give a gift to them in honor of my volunteer work.*

Or a possible request:

I encourage you to designate some or all of your gift to the volunteer department that is responsible for engaging hundreds of volunteers in our fight for _____."

Or a touch of humor:

I really don't need any new trinkets! I am too busy volunteering to dust them! Or, "No more ties! Remember I have retired from them."

(continued)

Gifts in Honor of Volunteers

(continued)

> *Please send your check to:* [Organization's name and contact info] *or go online at www.homelessshelterhaven.org and click: Gifts-in-Honor.*
>
> *I thank you and* [the clients of "The Shelter"] *send their deepest appreciation.*
>
> *Signature*
>
> *P.S. Another way you can honor me is to consider joining me as a volunteer... when the timing is good for you. It is truly my gift to you!*

Step 3

Develop a process for receiving and acknowledging donations. This may mean first notifying the volunteer that a donation has been made in his or her name. Create a method for responding to donors quickly and warmly. (The volunteer and the organization should respond.)

Step 4

Explain the program and distribute cards to all volunteers, including board members. Place more cards where people can find them all year long.

Step 5

At a designated time, evaluate the effectiveness of this method of generating resources.

Do I budget and seek funding for volunteer involvement with these actions?

1. I make certain that adequate volunteer program costs are included in the organization's annual budget.

   ☐ Yes ☐ No ☐ Sometimes ☐ Will now initiate ☐ Not relevant

2. I interpret the financial needs to support volunteers to the board of directors.

   ☐ Yes ☐ No ☐ Sometimes ☐ Will now initiate ☐ Not relevant

3. I contribute ideas to and endorse the case statement we make to donors and funders to support effective volunteer engagement.

   ☐ Yes ☐ No ☐ Sometimes ☐ Will now initiate ☐ Not relevant

4. I develop and support policies and protocol giving volunteers and appropriate former clients an opportunity to contribute financially to the organization.

   ☐ Yes ☐ No ☐ Sometimes ☐ Will now initiate ☐ Not relevant

5. I share stories of volunteer impact in presentations to the public, funders, and potential donors.

   ☐ Yes ☐ No ☐ Sometimes ☐ Will now initiate ☐ Not relevant

6. I allow some funds raised by volunteers to be earmarked to support the capacity of the organization to engage volunteers effectively.

   ☐ Yes ☐ No ☐ Sometimes ☐ Will now initiate ☐ Not relevant

7. I educate the organization's current and potential funders about the support needed to involve volunteers creatively and effectively.

   ☐ Yes ☐ No ☐ Sometimes ☐ Will now initiate ☐ Not relevant

8. I request recordkeeping and reports that identify the cross-over of volunteering and donating money to the organization.

   ☐ Yes ☐ No ☐ Sometimes ☐ Will now initiate ☐ Not relevant

Hiring and Placing Staff
to Lead Volunteer Engagement

> **"** *It takes investment in a staff position and reasonable funding to support the [volunteer] program; it can be time-consuming as the program grows but the rewards are far greater than the challenges.*
>
> **Dave Poulton, Executive Director**
> **Canadian Parks and**
> **Wilderness Society**
> **Calgary/Banff Chapter, Canada**

> *Hire the best volunteer manager you can find. This single factor has a huge impact on whether your program will succeed or fail. Be prepared to provide competitive salary and benefits, treat her or him as a manager, and make the investment of your time to keep your management of volunteer resources position from being a training position or a revolving door.* **"**
>
> **Jay Spradling**
> **Assistant Chief of Police**
> **Tempe Police Department**
> **Tempe, Arizona**

CONTENTS

- **Introduction** to the Executive Role

- **Key Concept:** Why Designate or Hire a Leader of Volunteer Involvement?

- **Key Concept:** Models of Staffing Volunteer Engagement

- **Checklist:** Potential Responsibilities of a Leader of Volunteer Involvement

- **Checklist:** Skills, Knowledge and Experience Needed to Be a Successful Leader of Volunteer Involvement

- **Idea Stimulator:** Considerations in Choosing a Title for the Leader of Volunteer Involvement

- **Idea Stimulator:** Considerations in Setting the Salary of the Leader of Volunteer Involvement

- **Idea Stimulator:** Considerations in Where to Place the Leader of Volunteer Involvement

- **Key Concept:** Why Place the Director of Volunteer Involvement on the Executive Management Team

- **Key Concept:** Places to Find Candidates for the Position of Director of Volunteer Involvement

- **Idea Stimulator:** Potential Interview Questions for Hiring a Director of Volunteer Involvement

- **Executive Self-Assessment:** *Do I hire and place the best person to lead volunteer engagement with these actions?*

CONCEPTS IN DEPTH   The tools in this section apply the concepts discussed at length in the book, *From the Top Down: The Executive Role in Successful Volunteer Involvement, 3rd edition,* by Susan J. Ellis (Philadelphia: Energize, Inc., 2010), specifically:

- Chapter 2: Considerations in Planning
- Chapter 4: Staffing Volunteer Involvement
- Appendix A: Volunteer Involvement Task Outline

||

Introduction to the Executive Role

The CEO volunteer champions in my 2005 study frequently noted that the action with the most significant impact on the success of their volunteer engagement strategy was hiring the right person to lead it (Stallings 2005).

There are two components to hiring a successful director of volunteer involvement. (You may choose a different title and we'll deal with that on page 85.) The first is to understand fully what the position is all about in order to define the work and be able to write an accurate job description. As executive, what do you expect from this critical staff member? Do you perceive the role as management or lower level? What should you require as qualifications and experience? Are you prepared to offer a salary commensurate with a highly skilled position? Will you place the person on your management team?

The second component to success is finding the best qualified person to fill this significant role. Where should you look? What questions should you ask in a screening interview?

Rarely are executive directors given tools to help them identify what the organization needs most in a leader of volunteer involvement and design or re-design that role to meet those needs. Here is the rationale for sequence and content of the materials contained in this unique section:

- If you or others in your organization are not yet convinced, you'll see how to make the case for hiring a director of volunteer involvement.

- Next is a presentation of the most common models of staffing volunteer engagement. You will need to choose which is most appropriate to meet the needs of your organization.

- Then comes a cluster of resources focused on articulating what you might include as you create or redesign the position of director of volunteer involvement. Specifically, you'll find:

  - A list of potential responsibilities
  - The range of skills and experience you might seek
  - Information explaining how the title, salary, and placement you assign to this position can support or undermine the other decisions
  - Considerations in where to place this position within the organization—pros and cons of different chains of authority
  - Why you should consider placing the director of volunteer involvement on your organization's executive management team

- You'll find some ideas on where to look for an experienced candidate, followed by a starter set of interview questions that will uncover a great deal about each applicant's perspective and skills in working with volunteers.

If you place the right person in this position, you will be well on your way to creating and sustaining mission-driven volunteer engagement.

Why Designate or Hire a Leader of Volunteer Involvement?

As with any organizational goal, the best way to ensure its success is to create a plan, allocate resources, and designate someone with responsibility to implement it. If you truly want effective volunteer involvement, you must assign a leader with proven skills to make it happen. The list below explains why you need someone (here called the *director of volunteer involvement*) to take the lead in developing, implementing, and overseeing your volunteer engagement strategy.

- Very few staff already on board have the time, interest, or training to develop volunteer engagement. If the responsibility is simply added on to someone's existing responsibilities, chances are it will not take priority. On the other hand, someone who genuinely wants to take on this role and is experienced in volunteer management will make volunteers the focus of attention, strategic planning, and creative thinking.

- If you want to have more volunteers contribute to your mission, recognize that more time and effort will be needed to recruit, train, and coordinate them, as well as preparing staff and building organizational readiness to put volunteer talents to work without wasting volunteer or employee time.

- A skilled, experienced director of volunteer involvement will set high standards in recruiting, screening, documenting, training, recognizing, and assessing the quality of service of volunteers.

- Because a designated director of volunteer involvement is paying attention to what volunteers do, she or he will limit risk by developing procedures for the safety and security of all concerned—and enforcing them.

- A director of volunteer involvement is constantly on the lookout for available community resources and will establish collaborative, mutually beneficial relationships between your organization and a wide range of local companies, schools, associations, and other talent pools—both to attract new volunteers and also to connect with potential donors of money and in-kind goods and services.

- Hiring someone who enthusiastically wants to be your director of volunteer involvement lowers the frequent turnover that plagues this role by having a person who is dedicated to the profession.

KEY CONCEPT

Models of Staffing Volunteer Engagement

> Depending on your organization's size, type, and stage of development, as well as what you want volunteers to accomplish and when, there are choices to be made in how to staff volunteer development. Lack of funds may influence your initial decision, but make it a goal to find funding as soon as possible for the staffing your organization really needs. Here are the major models:

Model 1:

The executive director, as head of the organization, leads the volunteer engagement effort and personally supervises volunteers as well as any paid staff.

Model 2:

The executive director designates a current staff member to implement volunteer involvement in addition to his or her job description, squeezing in time to do what is needed.

Model 3:

Someone is hired specifically as the leader of volunteer involvement on a part-time basis, with a focused-but-limited amount of time to devote to the responsibility.

Model 4:

The volunteer management function is decentralized in that *all* staff recruit and supervise volunteers working in their particular units or departments.

Model 5:

A full-time director of volunteer involvement is designated as the primary administrator of this function. The director of volunteer involvement may recruit and supervise all the organization's volunteers or (more common) the director of volunteer involvement recruits, screens, and orients volunteers, and then deploys them as needed to various departments or programs. Day-to-day supervision is given by frontline paid staff.

(continued)

Models of Staffing Volunteer Engagement
(continued)

Model 6:

Volunteers are self-led, generally organized with elected officers, committees, etc. (This model can exist side-by-side with other models.)

Model 7:

Administrative/clerical support is hired to support a full-time director because volunteer involvement has expanded beyond what one staff person can handle; more staff is also added as the volunteer corps grows.

As you select a model, keep in mind:

- There is no "best" method as there is not a one-size-fits-all way to staff volunteer engagement.

- Staffing should be assessed on a regular basis to determine if it is adequate to achieve volunteer involvement goals.

- Be careful of adding this work onto an already overloaded staff person who does not have the skills to fill this specialized role. It will not be that person's priority nor will you have a leader trained to do the work.

- Being a successful volunteer does not automatically translate into running the entire effort effectively. Do not hire a long-time volunteer to become the leader of volunteer engagement unless that person has the vision, skills, and experience to carry all the responsibilities.

- It *may* be possible to find a qualified volunteer to become your director of volunteer involvement without a salary. It is unlikely, however, that a volunteer can afford to take on this role for as many hours per week as are really needed, all year round, without some pay. But, if you do have such a special person available, be aware of potential problems of acceptance by other staff and be sure you validate the volunteer as a management-level team member.

- Be aware that the model you select might send a message about your willingness to designate resources to support volunteer involvement as well as the value your organization places on volunteers.

‖‖‖ ✔ ‖‖‖

CHECKLIST

Potential Responsibilities of a Leader of Volunteer Involvement

As you work on writing a job description for your designated leader of volunteer involvement, consider the functions and tasks below as a starter set of ideas. But don't be limited by them; your organization may have additional needs.

There are some functions that you will clearly expect from anyone in this position, which can be summarized in a long sentence such as: *Design, implement, and oversee the recruiting, screening, placing, orienting, and training process of volunteer applicants.* But be careful not to minimize what each of these elements of effective volunteer involvement requires in terms of activity. See appendix A in *From the Top Down* for a full task outline of the role of a director of volunteer involvement (Ellis 2010).

There are other, perhaps less obvious, responsibilities you might include in the position description for this role. Check off the responsibilities below to build a position description ideal for your organization.

☐ Bring a strong vision of and commitment to the value of volunteer participation.

☐ Recognize the wealth of untapped talents in the community that can be mobilized on our organization's behalf.

☐ In collaboration with management and staff, design and implement the organization's volunteer service structure (i.e., policy, lines of accountability, volunteer roles and opportunities) to meet the needs of the clients and achieve the organization's mission.

☐ Develop and maintain an effective and viable volunteer service base to meet organizational objectives.

☐ Prepare, negotiate, and monitor the financial resources required by the organization's volunteer service. Operate within approved budget guidelines and account for variances.

☐ Keep informed of current trends and standards of practice in the field of volunteer management.

(continued)

Potential Responsibilities of a Leader of Volunteer Involvement

(continued)

☐ Develop and maintain a positive and supportive working relationship with both internal and external stakeholders, from the board of directors to all levels of staff, and with community organizations.

☐ Provide appropriate support and training for staff responsible for supervising or partnering with the organization's volunteers.

☐ Foster an organizational environment in which volunteers are valued, supported, and recognized for their contributions to achieving the organization's mission.

☐ Represent volunteer involvement in the strategic planning of the organization.

☐ Establish and assess volunteer service goals and outcomes. Submit appropriate reports related to volunteer service activities and needs.

☐ Represent the organization in public speaking engagements and community relations events in the area of volunteerism.

☐ Act as the organization's professional expert in all matters concerning volunteers and volunteerism.

☐ Represent volunteer involvement on the organization's management team.

☐ Work with development staff to raise funds to support volunteer engagement

CHECKLIST

Skills, Knowledge, and Experience Needed to Be a Successful Leader of Volunteer Involvement

Leading volunteer involvement is a left brain/right brain activity. The person needs all sorts of interpersonal skills but must also be a solid administrator. Look over the list below and check off those that seem most appropriate for your organization's director of volunteer involvement.

Keep in mind that one person rarely can possess all of these skills. Think about what skills current staff already possess (and whether those staff members are in a position to partner with the director of volunteer involvement). Also, consider if volunteers with specific skills can be brought on board to support the director of volunteer involvement's role.

Interpersonal

- ☐ Interviewing
- ☐ Applying group dynamics techniques
- ☐ Influencing/persuading
- ☐ Managing conflict
- ☐ Supervising
- ☐ Delegating
- ☐ Coaching
- ☐ Managing change
- ☐ Welcoming/accommodating diversity

Creativity

- ☐ Graphic arts and design
- ☐ Promoting an energetic and motivating work environment

Communication

- ☐ Basic computer skills such as word processing, e-mailing and using the Internet for research
- ☐ Outreach via social media
- ☐ Written communication skills
- ☐ Public relations
- ☐ Public speaking
- ☐ Training design and delivery

Community Outreach

- ☐ Recruitment
- ☐ Media relations
- ☐ Coalition building
- ☐ Knowledge of community resources

Administrative

- ☐ Organizing/scheduling/coordinating
- ☐ Recordkeeping
- ☐ Task analysis and job design
- ☐ Budgeting and fiscal management
- ☐ Event planning
- ☐ Resource development
- ☐ Statistics
- ☐ Risk management
- ☐ Time management
- ☐ Program assessment
- ☐ Ability to use specific computer software for administrative tasks (e.g., Microsoft Excel)

☐ **Other:** _____

Considerations in Choosing a Title
for the Leader of Volunteer Involvement

The person who will lead volunteer engagement has a complex and critical role to fill, with responsibilities inside the organization and out in the community. Do you perceive the role as management or lower level? Will you offer a salary commensurate with a highly skilled position? Consider what you communicate to employees and volunteers by the choices you make in assigning a title, a salary, and a place in the organizational hierarchy to this leader.

1. Indicate the Level of Authority

- Use words such as *administrator, director, or manager* if…
  The position is responsible for administrative aspects of volunteer engagement for the entire organization (planning, budgeting, supervision, staff and volunteer leadership training, etc.). This title therefore places the person on the level of other department or unit heads who have comparable authority.

- Use the word *coordinator* if…
  The position mainly involves oversight of volunteers/activities or if the person primarily coordinates volunteer schedules throughout the organization.

2. Delineate the Focus of Responsibility

What or who is this staff member leading? A few choices for vocabulary are shown here, but you can be as creative as you wish to set the tone for the scope of community resource mobilization you most want:

- volunteers
- volunteer involvement
- volunteer engagement
- community resources
- community resource mobilization
- citizen participation
- community action

(continued)

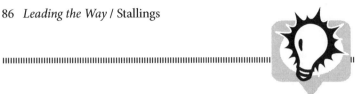

Considerations in Choosing a Title
for the Leader of Volunteer Involvement
(continued)

3. Examples

- director of volunteer involvement *(Note that I chose this title to use in this book.)*

- director of community resource mobilization

- coordinator of volunteers

- manager of community resources

4. Avoid Conflicting Titles

- **Avoid using "volunteer" as the first word of the title.**
  Make sure it is clear that volunteer is being used as a noun and not an adjective. A director of volunteers emphasizes the people being organized. But if the title is volunteer coordinator, there can be confusion as to whether or not this person is an unpaid leader of something (what?).

- **Avoid using "volunteer program" in the title.**
  Volunteer engagement is a method of service delivery, a fundamental human resource that partners with salaried staff in carrying out the mission in myriad ways. Using the term "volunteer program" sets the work of volunteers into a separate service, perhaps seen in competition with client-centered programs, when the goal is to enable volunteers to work wherever most needed throughout the agency.

- **If necessary, give the staff person two or more titles.**
  If a person holds several positions within the organization, as is often the case with directors of volunteer involvement, give that staff person two or more titled business cards to use when functioning in one or the other role.

Considerations in Setting the Salary of the Leader of Volunteer Involvement

The leader of volunteer engagement position has often been poorly paid, which has started a vicious cycle: highly skilled people are not attracted to low pay, so candidates for this important role tend to be inexperienced. Therefore, you may not find the skills and talent needed to perform this position well, and ultimately the potential of great volunteer involvement may never be achieved.

Avoid researching "comparable salaries" for other volunteer management positions in other agencies. As with other careers, salaries can differ between different industries. Instead, answer the following questions and draw your own conclusions as to what salary to offer in your organization and industry:

- At what level will this position be placed on our organizational chart? What are comparable salaries within the organization at that same level?

- What is the skill level required for this position? What salary will attract excellent applicants? Low salaries will perpetuate hiring a poorly qualified person leading to less successful volunteer engagement and high turnover (which is costly in itself). Select a candidate with the appropriate skills, training, and experience. It may cost a bit more but should bring a better return on investment than an unskilled hire.

- Although a seasoned volunteer may be very familiar with your organization and an outstanding service provider, success as a frontline volunteer does not automatically translate into being a successful leader of other volunteers. The candidate must be a successful and motivated worker as well as a superb delegator, motivator, and organizer. They must be able to empower others to be successful. If a current volunteer fits that description, great! Otherwise, be sure to select the person with the right skills, training, and experience.

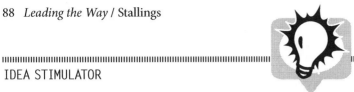

Considerations in Where to Place the Leader of Volunteer Involvement

There is no definite right or wrong department or level in the organization in which to place the director of volunteer involvement (referred to as DVI below), but the choice should be made strategically. Below are some of the most common options, with some pros and cons of each placement site.

DVI Placed in this Dept. or Office	Pros	Cons
Executive Offices (reporting directly to the executive director)	• Sends a powerful message as to the value placed on volunteer engagement • DVI continually has overview of the whole organization, as well as access to any staff member	• Lower level staff may feel constrained from sharing concerns or needs • Executive may divert the DVI to other areas/activities unrelated to volunteer engagement
Human Resources or Personnel	• DVI will be seen as the human resource specialist for non-paid staff • Can merge some systems for creating position descriptions, policies, employee handbooks, training, and recordkeeping	• Volunteers can easily be given lower priority than paid staff • HR responds to specific staff needs and within allocated budget, while a DVI can and should be proactive in developing many new roles for volunteers, and doesn't need to wait for funding
Development or Fundraising	• Seen internally and externally as part of the department that coordinates outreach to community groups and businesses, bringing in all community resources (both human and financial) to further the mission of the organization	• No direct involvement with the service delivery staff, yet needs to place volunteers into all units • Not seen as a partner in resource development, but rather as an assistant to the person bringing in money • Volunteers may get the message that they are wanted for their financial value only
A specific client service, program, or unit	• The particular unit benefits from a strong volunteer component	• Can be buried in one unit with little opportunity for widespread engagement throughout the organization

(continued)

Considerations in Where to Place
the Leader of Volunteer Involvement
(continued)

DVI Placed in this Dept. or Office	Pros	Cons
Public/ Community Relations or Marketing	• Sends message that volunteers are key in positive public relations • DVI has support in media relations, technology, graphic arts, and other elements important in recruiting and recognizing volunteers	• No direct involvement with the service delivery staff, yet needs to place volunteers into all units • Can seem as if volunteers are "for show" rather than engaged in substantive ways
A separate Volunteer Involvement Department	• DVI seen as a department head and serves on the senior management team • Volunteers recognized as vital enough to warrant focused attention from the top of the organization	• Staff can feel that volunteers "belong" to a separate department, when, in fact, everyone is responsible for supporting volunteers • Other department heads may not understand the need for the DVI to be involved in daily operations

Why Place the Director of Volunteer Involvement on the Executive Management Team

- Placing the director of volunteer involvement on the management team is the strongest way an organization can say, "We value the essential contributions of volunteers and value the input of the leader of volunteer engagement in all planning and discussions related to achieving our mission."

- When the director of volunteer involvement is on the management team, that person has equal footing with other key leaders in the organization.

- The director of volunteer involvement is the person on staff who can help the organization think carefully and creatively about: 1) integrating volunteer engagement throughout the organization; 2) new opportunities to engage citizens in the mission; and 3) cautions and risk issues to protect volunteers, the clients, and the organization.

- Staff are more likely to accept volunteer involvement if senior leaders contribute to its design, evaluation, future vision, and more. As part of the management team, the director of volunteer involvement can ensure that they do so.

- Participation on the management team enables the director of volunteer involvement to be actively involved and knowledgeable about all organizational issues and can better advise how volunteers can contribute to these issues.

- The director of volunteer involvement may annually oversee more people than any other person on the staff and thus needs the best information possible to direct programs and respond to volunteer issues and concerns.

- The director of volunteer involvement must often influence frontline staff over whom they have no control. Other department managers will more likely understand and respect the role the director of volunteer involvement plays in placing and supporting volunteers throughout the organization when she or he is on the management team.

- Staff experiencing problems as they work with volunteers can sabotage volunteer engagement if staff see no resolution of these issues. These situations are difficult to diagnose and respond to unless the director of volunteer involvement sits on the management team and has frequent contact with staff leadership.

Places to Find Candidates for the Position of Director of Volunteer Involvement

Because there are so many variations of volunteer involvement leadership, including a wide range of position titles, it is not always easy to locate people with relevant experience to become your director of volunteer involvement. The following resources may be of great help in advertising your job opening but may not be available or may have different titles outside North America.

Online Resources

- There are a number of Web sites with job banks (many will post job openings at no charge) that focus on or include position openings in volunteer management. Three examples are listed below. The first two list jobs in any country.

    - Energize, Inc. (http://www.energizeinc.com/jobs.html)

    - Idealist (http://www.idealist.org/if/as/Job)

    - The NonProfit Times (http://www.nptimes.com/careers.html)

- Online discussion groups for people already in volunteer management jobs, including the following:

    - CyberVPM (http://groups.yahoo.com/group/cybervpm/)

    - OzVPM (http://groups.yahoo.com/group/ozvpm)

    - UKVPMs (http://www.onelist.com/community/UKVPMs)

Professional Associations

Volunteer management practitioners form professional societies, as do other mutual-interest groups. Clearly, here is where you can find experienced candidates for your new position, including people currently in assistant roles who are ready for greater responsibility.

- At the local level, a community may have what is generically called a "DOVIA" (Directors of Volunteers in Agencies) group. They can have one of many different names. Look for your local DOVIA at http://www.energizeinc.com/prof/dovia.html .

(continued)

Places to Find Candidates for the
Position of Director of Volunteer Involvement
(continued)

- There are state and provincial associations of volunteerism and affinity group associations, such as directors of volunteer resources in health care, museums, local government, and more.

- Find practitioners who have earned their CVA designation, Certified in Volunteer Administration, from the Council on Certification in Volunteer Administration, http://www.cvacert.org.

- In larger cities, you may find a Corporate Volunteer Council, which is a professional association for employees of larger businesses charged with running their companies' employee volunteer programs. For more information on Corporate Volunteer Councils, go to http://www.handsonnetwork.org/companies/corporatevolunteercouncils.

- Also consider contacting professional societies for related fields, including: human resources, fundraising, special event planning, alumni office leadership, and other settings.

Volunteerism Resource Centers

All of the following communicate regularly with their constituents and therefore can publicize job openings in some way, and often can give personal recommendations as well.

- Local, regional, state or provincial volunteer centers and other clearinghouses of volunteer opportunities. Can have many names, such as HandsOn Action Centers, State Associations of Volunteer Centers, etc.

- State or provincial offices of volunteer resources: government units that monitor and facilitate volunteer involvement in the nonprofit sector.

Other Sources

- College and university programs offering academic degrees, certificates, and noncredit workshops in nonprofit management, philanthropy, public administration, and volunteer management.

- Management Assistance Programs offering courses in volunteer management.

Potential Interview Questions
for Hiring a Director of Volunteer Involvement

After you have determined the skills, qualities, and experiences you are looking for in your director of volunteer involvement, create questions that will explore each candidate's capability in those designated skills and qualities. The following are some beginning thoughts and examples, with continuing thanks to Grant McEwan University in Edmonton, Alberta, Canada, for the unattributed original series of questions obtained there almost twenty years ago and refined over time:

Experience and Philosophy of Volunteering

- What volunteer work have you personally done? What did the organization do well (or not well) to support your work as a volunteer?

- What is your personal philosophy of volunteering? (Suggestion: You may ask candidates to write this and bring it to the interview. It will also be a way to see candidates' writing style/ability.)

- Do you consider student interns to be volunteers? What about court-referred workers?

- Why do you feel organizations such as ours should engage volunteers?

Knowledge of Community Resources

- How familiar are you with community organizations, faith communities, civic clubs, service organizations, and the Chamber of Commerce in our area of service? If not, how will you go about making connections with them?

- Have you ever developed or been a participant in a group of volunteer advocates who speak about your issue, opportunities to serve, etc., to groups in the community? What were the challenges of this endeavor and what were the noted outcomes/impact?

Communication Skills (Oral and Written)

- Describe the most challenging situation in which you presented information (oral and/or in writing) to an individual or group.

- How did you present it and what was the response?

- What did you learn from this experience?

(continued)

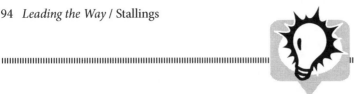

Potential Interview Questions
for Hiring a Director of Volunteer Involvement
(continued)

- What experience have you had recruiting volunteers?

- What are the most successful/least successful approaches you have used?

- What are some key interview questions to ask volunteers about their interest in becoming volunteers?

Interpersonal Skills

- Describe a project where you had to work with other stakeholders (staff, colleagues, or volunteers) and one of those stakeholders did not follow through with their task/commitment. What did you do? What was the outcome?

- What has been your experience in working with people of different ages and a variety of backgrounds?

- If you encounter resistance to volunteers from any paid staff member, how would you handle it?

- How do you plan to maintain contact with colleagues in your field over the next year?

Diplomacy/Advocacy Skills

- Describe a situation where you had to confront or discipline a volunteer who had a performance problem. What was the situation, how did you handle it and what was the outcome?

- Describe a situation in which you advocated for an issue or cause. What did you do and what was the result?

Strategic Planning Skills

- Describe an event you planned that involved the community for which you met the goals, objectives, and timelines? What methods do you use to stay on task and to monitor the work of others?

- What kind of documentation and evaluation systems have you implemented? How have they affected your strategic planning?

(continued)

Potential Interview Questions
for Hiring a Director of Volunteer Involvement
(continued)

Organizational Skills

- Often our workplace can be chaotic. How do you prioritize your workload to meet organizational objectives and goals?

- In what ways have you contributed to the personal or professional development of colleagues (volunteers and staff) in previous work environments? How did you recognize that "change" or "development" was needed? What processes were put into place to ensure these needs were addressed?

Analytical Reasoning/Problem Solving

- How and where do you find information to keep abreast of changing standards of practice, legal requirements, and new approaches to effective volunteer management?

- Please describe when you tested a new concept or model related to your work. What problems or barriers did you encounter? What was the outcome of this experiment?

Creativity

- What is the most creative way you have recruited volunteers?

- What ways have you creatively recognized volunteers?

Decision-Making Skills

- Leaders of volunteer involvement are constantly making decisions based on policy or procedures or, at other times, based on instinct. Have you ever had the experience of turning down a volunteer who wanted to work at your organization? What decision-making process did you use to come to that decision?

Ethical Practice and Professionalism

- What ethical issues have you faced in your previous experience as a manager of volunteer engagement? (Suggestion: You may wish to explore issues such as unions, confidentiality, boundaries, risk management, exploitation of volunteers.)

(continued)

Potential Interview Questions
for Hiring a Director of Volunteer Involvement
(continued)

- What do you identify as the primary responsibilities of the manager of volunteer resources? What experiences do you have in these areas?

Training

- What experience have you had in designing orientation sessions and/or in providing training for volunteers or for staff who partner with volunteers?

- How will you approach/handle this responsibility at our organization?

- What have you found to be the greatest challenges in training?

Delegation

- The responsibility of managing the volunteer program is extensive. What parts of the role might you delegate to a volunteer to carry out and report to you?

- How have you modeled good delegation in past jobs and/or volunteer experiences? What have been the challenges? How have you handled them? Particularly if you are a high achiever, what have you learned about your own capability to effectively delegate? How have you worked through any hesitancy to share work with volunteers?

- How would you define a good manager? Do you personally prefer doing work directly with clients or supporting/empowering other people to be successful at a task/job?

Computer and Internet Technology

- What is your comfort level and experience in using the Internet and in electronic means of communicating, training, etc.?

- How do you feel that technology is/can enhance volunteer involvement efforts?

- What is your familiarity with social media? What are some ways it could be used to enhance volunteer involvement?

(continued)

Potential Interview Questions
for Hiring a Director of Volunteer Involvement
(continued)

Diversity

- The position of director of volunteer involvement is one that interfaces with people with a very wide range in ages, capabilities, positions and ethnic and other diverse backgrounds. What has been your experience in dealing with a wide gamut of people? What have been your greatest challenges with this and how have you developed sensitivity and capability to interface with all types of people?

Situational Questions

One technique that is particularly useful in interviewing is to explore the response of a candidate to a situation that can occur on the job. Describe an incident that has occurred with volunteers in your organizations and ask how the applicant might have handled it. Some examples:

- A volunteer/major donor who is asking for special privileges

- Talking to staff who are not adequately supporting the volunteers they supervise

- Dealing with a volunteer whose motives for volunteering are in conflict with your organization's values, etc.

As you interview...

Listen and watch for evidence of the qualities needed in a director of volunteer involvement, including:

- Warmth

- Friendliness

- Flexibility

- Creativity

- Energy

Do I hire and place the best person to lead volunteer engagement with these actions?

1. I am a proponent of creating a budget line to support a director of volunteer involvement's position as the person's primary job, even if it is part time.

   ☐ Yes   ☐ No   ☐ Sometimes   ☐ Will now initiate   ☐ Not relevant

2. I understand the variety of models to carry out volunteer management and strive to obtain the one best suited to our organization's needs and capability.

   ☐ Yes   ☐ No   ☐ Sometimes   ☐ Will now initiate   ☐ Not relevant

3. Since the director of volunteer involvement does not have authority over people he/she needs to influence, I make sure that all staff and volunteers understand the role and responsibilities of the person holding this position.

   ☐ Yes   ☐ No   ☐ Sometimes   ☐ Will now initiate   ☐ Not relevant

4. I make certain that all staff are apprised of the roles they play in supporting volunteer engagement within our organization.

   ☐ Yes   ☐ No   ☐ Sometimes   ☐ Will now initiate   ☐ Not relevant

5. I recommend placement of the director of volunteer involvement in the best location of the organization's structure to ensure volunteerism is integrated throughout the organization.

   ☐ Yes   ☐ No   ☐ Sometimes   ☐ Will now initiate   ☐ Not relevant

6. I monitor the growth and impact of volunteer involvement as an indicator of a time for expansion of staff support for it.

   ☐ Yes   ☐ No   ☐ Sometimes   ☐ Will now initiate   ☐ Not relevant

7. I make certain that the position title and salary is aligned with the skills, experience, responsibilities, and expectations of the position and is aligned in salary and placement in relation to other staff positions.

   ☐ Yes   ☐ No   ☐ Sometimes   ☐ Will now initiate   ☐ Not relevant

(continued)

Do I hire and place the best person to lead volunteer engagement with these actions?

(continued)

8. Before hiring a director of volunteer involvement, I determine the competencies needed to carry out the position and, if appropriate, review questions for interviewing candidates.

   ☐ Yes   ☐ No   ☐ Sometimes   ☐ Will now initiate   ☐ Not relevant

9. I place the director of volunteer involvement on the management team or, minimally, create opportunities for exchange of information and input for her/him with executive leadership of the organization.

   ☐ Yes   ☐ No   ☐ Sometimes   ☐ Will now initiate   ☐ Not relevant

Creating a Management Team
for Volunteer Involvement

CONTENTS

- **Introduction** to the Executive Role

- **Self-Inquiry:** Assessing Organizational Team Culture: How We Support Volunteer Involvement

- **Key Concept:** The Case for Initiating a Management Team for Volunteer Involvement

- **Action Steps:** Developing a Management Team for Volunteer Involvement

- **Idea Stimulator:** Potential Challenges in Building a Successful Management Team for Volunteer Involvement

- **Executive Self-Assessment:** *Do I create and sustain management team support for volunteer involvement with these actions?*

CONCEPTS
IN DEPTH

The tools in this section apply the concepts discussed at length in the book, *From the Top Down: The Executive Role in Successful Volunteer Involvement, 3rd edition,* by Susan J. Ellis (Philadelphia: Energize, Inc., 2010), specifically:

- Chapter 2: Considerations in Planning

||||||||||||||||||||||||||||||||||||||||||||||||||||||||||||||||||||||||||||||||||||||||||||||||||||||||||||||||||||||||||||||||||||||||||||||||||||||||

Introduction to the Executive Role

In many organizations, departments or units carry out their function(s) in silos despite the great advantage of collaborating and supporting one another. Also, the director of volunteer involvement rarely has direct authority over employees in other departments and so can meet resistance when expecting staff to partner effectively with volunteers.

The only way for volunteers to be truly integrated throughout the organization is for *all* staff to be involved in designing and sustaining volunteer involvement. Having a *management team* of key stakeholders helps accomplish organization-wide input and adds additional authority figures to help the director of volunteer involvement reach all staff. However, establishing the management team approach to involving volunteers requires initiative or strong support from the executive, setting the tone that volunteers are *everyone's* business.

Three models exist for team management of volunteer involvement:

1. **A Volunteer Involvement Advisory Council:** Generally composed of volunteers and staff who meet on a regular basis to give advice or carry out activities needed by the volunteer department, but who generally do not have the power or influence to act on their suggestions. This group is generally convened and supported by the director of volunteer involvement.

2. **The Organization's Senior Management Team:** Comprised of highest-level executives who can discuss issues relevant to the entire organization, including volunteer engagement, with authority to act on decisions they make. The director of volunteer involvement should serve on this team but is too often left out, forced to depend on the executive (or the person to whom she or he reports) to represent the volunteer viewpoint at senior management meetings.

3. **A Management Team for Volunteer Involvement:** A gathering of executives, key staff, board members, and leadership volunteers who have an interest in the success of volunteer engagement and the skills and power to support recommendations coming from the group.

This section focuses creating the third model, a management team for volunteer involvement, and examines how to ensure *management level* support of volunteer engagement. The section includes a self-inquiry to look at the organization's overall team culture, arguments for developing a management team to support volunteer engagement, steps for establishing that management team, and general challenges when doing so.

> *"...establishing the management team approach...requires initiative or strong support from the executive, setting the tone that volunteers are everyone's business."*

Assessing Organizational Team Culture: How We Support Volunteer Involvement

> In each section, check the description that best describes your organization.

1. How we function in general as team players in our organization:

☐ Currently we do not have a culture of team management within our organization. Departments work mostly independently, not interacting with one another.

☐ There are some collaborative efforts within our organization, but overall we operate as separate services, programs, and projects.

☐ We function well as a team and our plans and strategies are shared and in sync with one another.

☐ We are so team oriented that it is often hard to move forward and get consensus on actions we need to take.

☐ *None of the above. This is how I would describe our organization's team culture, in general:* _____

2. How we function as a team to support volunteer engagement:

a. In a small organization

☐ The functions of managing volunteer involvement are shared among our small staff but volunteers are not a clear priority for anyone.

☐ The functions of managing volunteer involvement are shared among our small staff, and we regularly devote time to planning for volunteer participation, allocating tasks to each other as necessary.

☐ One of our staff members has been designated to oversee and lead volunteer involvement on a part-time basis. All staff partner with volunteers assigned to them, but there is no planned team effort to ensure the most strategic and successful participation of volunteers.

(continued)

Assessing Organizational Team Culture: How We Support Volunteer Involvement

(continued)

☐ One of our staff members has been designated to oversee and lead volunteer involvement on a part-time basis. All staff, including our executive, work as a team to support effective engagement of volunteers.

☐ We expect to designate or hire a full-time leader of volunteer involvement if our organization expands or the volunteer corps grows to where it is necessary.

☐ We have designated a full-time person to lead volunteer engagement because volunteers are vital to carrying out our mission.

☐ *None of the above. This is how I would describe our team culture, as it relates to support of volunteers:*_____

b. In a mid-size to large organization

☐ The staff member who leads the organization's volunteer engagement does not sit on the organization's management team and is expected to carry out the work of volunteer engagement with minimal support from other staff/executives.

☐ The staff member who leads the organization's volunteer engagement sits on the management team of the organization. The team does deal with issues related to the volunteers but volunteerism is not considered essential and is often seen in competition with other "programs" of the organization. As a result, tangible support for volunteers is often found on the cutting block during tight times.

☐ The staff member who leads the organization's volunteer engagement sits on the management team of the organization. The team considers volunteers a vital component of the organization's operation and allocates appropriate time and resources to supporting volunteers.

☐ We have a strong ethic of team management and the director of volunteer involvement is a significant contributing member of the team.

☐ *None of the above. This is how I would describe our team culture, as it relates to support of volunteers:*_____

(continued)

Assessing Organizational Team Culture: How We Support Volunteer Involvement

(continued)

Questions to Ponder
Based on Your Responses to the Choices Above

1. What changes do you think our organization could make to move toward improving our team culture for supporting volunteer engagement?

2. What role can I play to promote these changes?

The Case for Initiating a
Management Team for Volunteer Involvement

> A **Management Team for Volunteer Involvement** is an ongoing gathering
> or task force of executive(s), key staff, board members and leadership vol-
> unteers who have an interest in the success of volunteer engagement and
> the skills and power to support recommendations coming from the group.
> Listed below are some arguments as to why such a team needed.

- Volunteers contribute considerable time, resources, and money toward the mission of the organization. So, it is incumbent upon top management to provide leadership and support to assure that the potential of volunteer contributions is maximized in all functions and units of the organization.

- Upper management and the board are the only ones who can create policy, generate resources, endorse/require training, and enforce standards about volunteer engagement and thus need to collaborate with the director of volunteer involvement to encourage all staff to understand and respect the importance of volunteer work.

- In section four is a presentation of the case for why a director of volunteer involvement ought to be on an organization's senior management team (see page 90). The senior management team will spend some time on the subject of volunteer engagement but, of necessity, deals with major agency-wide concerns, often in crisis, and may not be able to give adequate attention to issues related to ongoing volunteer management. Therefore, a team devoted to volunteer involvement can ensure volunteer involvement is getting attention on a regular basis.

- Since upper management is most informed about the organization's priorities and strategic plans, they are in the best position to incorporate goals for volunteer involvement that support the organization's overall mission, and a team approach ensures that they communicate those goals to staff responsible for mobilizing volunteers.

- Directors of volunteer involvement generally have no direct authority over most staff who must be influenced to work effectively with volunteers. Likewise, directors of volunteer involvement have no control over upper management who establish agency vision and priorities. Therefore, there is a need

(continued)

The Case for Initiating a
Management Team for Volunteer Involvement

(continued)

for those with authority and power to be strong advocates and supporters of volunteer engagement. This can be best achieved by a management team that focuses on issues of volunteer engagement and its implications for accomplishing the mission of the organization.

- Without management input, volunteer engagement will be little understood, appreciated or integrated into overall organization planning, thus considerably limiting the potential impact volunteers could make.

- The management team approach helps to clarify roles and responsibilities around volunteer management for all departments and staff, as well as defining the specific responsibilities of the director of volunteer involvement.

- A management team offers the opportunity of fresh ideas from people who do not usually take the time to think strategically about volunteers yet are in positions that can make a difference in how volunteers are welcomed and engaged.

- There is much more buy-in to volunteer engagement when managers are involved in the planning for and evaluation of volunteers. Such buy-in becomes contagious, winning over others to see benefits of effective volunteer involvement. Volunteer engagement cannot sit on the shoulders of one person (i.e., the director of volunteer involvement).

- A management team is a good place to discuss problems and concerns that may become barriers to involving volunteers in the future, if not resolved.

- Creative ways to approach everything, from recruitment and recognition to new placements of volunteers, more often emerge in an atmosphere of team spirit and synergy.

- Relationships formed during management team meetings will carry over to day-to-day working partnerships between the director of volunteer involvement and other staff, executives, and the board.

Developing a Management Team
for Volunteer Involvement

Step 1

Define the Team

This may need to be re-assessed annually and will vary considerably depending on whether this is a new effort to engage volunteers or one that has been in place for a while.

► *Expectations:* Will this team be:

- Advisory: talk only?
- Decision-making?
- Working: members to do tasks between meetings?
- A combination of the above?

► *Purpose:* What are the major purposes and priorities of the team? On what will they spend their time focusing? Some choices are:

- Create a vision and plan for a volunteer engagement strategy
- Develop the organization's philosophy of volunteer involvement
- Strengthen the overall effectiveness of volunteers in the organization
- Assess the impact of volunteer engagement on the organization's mission
- Identify new ways to engage volunteers
- Clarify roles and responsibilities of all staff in supporting volunteer engagement
- Create a volunteer-friendly organization that is also staff-friendly

► *Name:* Select a name that expresses the purpose of the group so that the rest of the organization understands the team's purpose and realizes the importance placed on engaging volunteers.

► *Duration:* Decide if the team will be:

- A time-limited task force (often the best choice when first initiating an executive team approach)
- A subcommittee of any existing management team already operating for the organization

(continued)

Developing a Management Team for Volunteer Involvement
(continued)

- An ongoing, stand-alone group (usually decided after positive impact of an initial task force)

Step 2

Determine the Level of Executive Involvement

Executive attention to significant volunteer issues is crucial to the success of volunteer engagement. Options for executive involvement with the management team include:

- Being a regular participating member of the team

- Designating a high-ranking deputy to represent executive management at all team meetings

- Engaging in written or in-person dialogue on issues discussed at the meetings

- Asking the board chair to assign a board member to sit on the team and then present issues to both the executive and the board

Step 3

Select the Team Members

► *Context:* Who should serve on the team will be determined by the organization's size, management culture, and existing support of volunteer involvement. Also, membership criteria may evolve over time as various topics or issues surface and are studied. But, as a general rule, participants on the team should be those paid staff and board members who:

- Have the greatest need or desire for volunteer engagement to be successful

- Are able to see a wider perspective beyond a single unit or department

- Can effectively articulate needs

- Have (or have a direct connection to) the power and resources to support changes and improvements recommended

(continued)

Developing a Management Team for Volunteer Involvement
(continued)

► Possible members include:

- Executive director or other executive staff member

- A member of the board of directors or someone representing the governing legislative body

- Department heads or unit supervisors of direct services to consumers

- Development director

- Event coordinator

- Personnel or human resources director

- Marketing and public relations staff

- Information technology manager or webmaster

- The director of volunteer involvement or staff person designated to provide leadership to volunteer engagement.

Step 4

Determine How the Team Will Do Its Work

► Discuss and make decisions about:

- Who will lead (chair) the team?

- If the director of volunteer involvement is not the chair, what will be his or her role on the team?

- How often will the team meet?

- Who will develop the agenda and how?

- What communication will be expected between meetings, and how?

- How will we hold members accountable for activities assigned to them?

- How will we deal with conflict, different opinions of members, etc.?

- How will we keep individuals motivated to contribute to team goals?

- How will we evaluate whether the team is effective?

(continued)

Developing a Management Team for Volunteer Involvement
(continued)

Step 5

Select Goals and Activities for the Team

Help the team to expand its vision of the potential of volunteer engagement by providing an orientation about current trends in volunteering today, including emerging sources of volunteers, new ways of designing work for volunteers, and more.

The goals and activities of the team will grow naturally out of its purpose, and should be re-defined annually. Some activities may be accomplished by one person or a designated task force rather than all team members doing every activity. Some potential goals/activities include:

- Drafting a philosophy statement for the organization's partnership with volunteers

- Assessing the volunteer trends (internal and external) that influence effective mobilization of volunteers

- Carrying out an agency assessment of volunteer engagement

- Gaining input from current and past volunteers regarding satisfaction with their volunteer involvement in the organization

- Determining staff barriers to effective volunteer engagement and initiating new ways to build commitment and deal with the challenges staff face

- Designing training for all staff who are involved in partnering with volunteers

- Setting goals to overcome some weaknesses or take advantage of emerging opportunities

- Promoting more extensive involvement of volunteers throughout the organization

- Developing volunteer positions that enhance the attainment of the organization's strategic goals

- Designing ways to engage volunteers in new roles such as consultants, entrepreneurs, or technical assistants, and in new assignments such as short-term, one-day, or virtual (online), and more

- Reviewing and updating policies in areas such as risk management

(continued)

Developing a Management Team for Volunteer Involvement
(continued)

- Clarifying the roles, responsibilities, and needed resources for staff involved in carrying out the elements of successful volunteer involvement

Step 6

Implement the Plans

- Develop goals, action plans, time lines, assignments, support, and the budget to accomplish the activities agreed upon.

Step 7

Evaluate the Impact of the Team

After a sufficient period of time has passed, the team needs to ask and answer the following questions:

► Did this team effort create a significant and positive impact on volunteer engagement?

- Were the stated goals of the team met and what was its impact?
- (If appropriate) was a new volunteer engagement plan initiated with positive support and involvement of staff?
- Is there now higher volunteer and staff satisfaction with volunteer participation?
- Is the organization becoming more staff- or volunteer-friendly as a result of the team's activities?

► Was it a good investment of team members' time to engage in this effort?

- Did the time invested in this team strengthen staff commitment and competency to partner with volunteers?
- Were meetings well attended and staff responsive to ideas and actions to improve volunteer involvement?
- Did participating team members develop a stronger understanding and investment in the potential power of volunteer engagement when well executed?
- Did team members feel that they were acknowledged for the time they invested in this team endeavor?

Potential Challenges in Building a Successful Management Team for Volunteer Involvement

As with any other team effort, it's best to be prepared to address any issues with potential to diminish progress towards the team's goals. Listed below are some common challenges. **How will you plan to avoid them?**

- **Poor use of time.** No one has time to waste. If the volunteer management team does not run efficient meetings participants will find reasons not to participate in this endeavor.

- **Lack of obvious benefits from the effort.** Tied to efficient use of time is effective use of time. Team members need to see results and know that their participation is making a difference.

- **Insufficient initial discussion on how the team will operate, make decisions, etc.** Lack of clear direction/action will be frustrating to participants.

- **Unclear expectations.** Members did not know what they were agreeing to, such as whether the team is temporary or ongoing, or how much time it would take. If the work of the team extends beyond original expectations, there will be resentment, followed by lack of follow through by participants.

- **No team agreement on the basics.** Finding that every team member has a different definition of what a volunteer is and should do will make group decision making nearly impossible. Without agreement on the definition and role of volunteers, individual members will have very different perspectives on suggested actions impacting volunteer involvement.

- **Inadequate leadership.** The person running the meeting is not prepared or in control. This is an opportunity for the director of volunteer involvement to show professionalism and run a great meeting. But if another member of the team has more ability in meeting management, that person should facilitate the group in accomplishing the agenda. Also, the other team members need to recognize and be on board with who the team leader is.

- **Ineffective communication between meetings.** Significant information needs to be shared with members to keep them up to date on progress, actions, or key responses team members are experiencing. On the other hand, if there is too much unnecessary information shared, members will begin to ignore communications from other team members.

(continued)

Potential Challenges in Building a Successful Management Team for Volunteer Involvement
(continued)

- **No recorded minutes.** No one is keeping track of action taken or agreed-upon tasks between meetings. At the first meeting, it should be decided who will keep a record of actions taken, assignments made, time lines agreed to, etc.

- **Members are not held accountable for following through on their assignments.** At the first meeting, the convener needs to lead some discussion about the significance of people carrying through on assignments accepted. When an assignment is delegated, the convener needs to ask what support/resources are needed to carry out the activity.

- **Few resources available to carry out suggestions.** If resources are not available, finding/generating them should become a first action step.

- **High member turnover, causing lack of continuity and institutional memory.** If team members are not required to serve on the volunteer management team and there is no benefit to service, there is apt to be high turnover rate of participants who believe that other issues hold greater significance in the organization.

- **Poor meeting attendance.** If no one comes to the table, nothing can be accomplished. Generally, members won't attend meetings due to some of the problems already listed above. If attendance becomes a problem, the team leader or executive must deal with it immediately as it will undermine the effectiveness of the team.

- **Sending representatives to meetings.** The executives on the team must understand that only they have the authority to make decisions. If a member cannot attend personally, any substitute representative must bring that executive's views to the table and have the authority to vote in his or her place.

- **Statistical analysis leading to paralysis.** There will never be 100 percent surety of anything, and there is rarely good data to help in making decisions about volunteers. On the other hand, some team members will not be prone to extensive analysis before recommending action. Find a happy medium that permits knowledgeable and timely decision making.

- **Little or no response from the top.** If the executive is a member of the team, he or she needs to carry through with decisions made. If decisions must be reported to a higher level for approval and action, responses must come in a timely and supportive fashion or the strategies of the team will not move

Do I create and sustain management team support for volunteer involvement with these actions?

1. Overall, my leadership style promotes a team approach to decision making and planning.

   ☐ Yes   ☐ No   ☐ Sometimes   ☐ Will now initiate   ☐ Not relevant

2. I have encouraged, initiated, or supported an involved and effective management team to lead our volunteer engagement effort.

   ☐ Yes   ☐ No   ☐ Sometimes   ☐ Will now initiate   ☐ Not relevant

3. I serve on (or give regular input to) the management team that discusses volunteer involvement (or I have a representative who brings the executive perspective to such discussions).

   ☐ Yes   ☐ No   ☐ Sometimes   ☐ Will now initiate   ☐ Not relevant

4. I encourage the involvement of a board member to serve on the management team for volunteer involvement.

   ☐ Yes   ☐ No   ☐ Sometimes   ☐ Will now initiate   ☐ Not relevant

5. I require participation of key staff to serve on the volunteer management team and show appreciation for their contributions to creating/sustaining effective volunteer engagement.

   ☐ Yes   ☐ No   ☐ Sometimes   ☐ Will now initiate   ☐ Not relevant

6. Recommendations made by the management team about volunteer engagement are respectfully considered in a timely fashion by me or other appropriate executive(s) in the organization.

   ☐ Yes   ☐ No   ☐ Sometimes   ☐ Will now initiate   ☐ Not relevant

7. If appropriate, I recommend that the person designated to provide leadership to our volunteer engagement sit on the senior management team of the entire organization.

   ☐ Yes   ☐ No   ☐ Sometimes   ☐ Will now initiate   ☐ Not relevant

8. I encourage a yearly staff team review of the impact of volunteer involvement on our mission.

   ☐ Yes   ☐ No   ☐ Sometimes   ☐ Will now initiate   ☐ Not relevant

Building Staff Commitment and Competency to Partner with Volunteers

> **E**xpectations for working with volunteers are spelled out when we hire new staff, in job descriptions and during performance evaluations.

Roberta Downey,
Executive Director
Eastern Agency on Aging
Bangor, Maine

We have clear expectations of staff for supervising volunteers and provide staff with appropriate recognition for excellence in this area.

Stacy C. James, CEO
Intermountain Planned
Parenthood
Billings, Montana

CONTENTS

- **Introduction** to the Executive Role

- **Self-Inquiry:** Executive Perspective on Strengthening Staff Partnerships with Volunteers

- **Survey:** Assessing Staff Commitment to Partner with Volunteers

- **Checklist:** How Executives Ensure that All Staff Are Clear on What Is Expected from Them in Working with Volunteers

- **Idea Stimulator:** Staff Actions in Partnering with Volunteers

- **Example:** Staff Actions in Partnering with Volunteers

- **Idea Stimulator:** Building Staff Competence through Training

- **Survey:** Determining Staff Training Needs for Working with Volunteers

- **Idea Stimulator:** Ways to Show Appreciation for Staff Excellence in Partnering with Volunteers

- **Executive Self-Assessment:** *Do I ensure staff commitment and competency in volunteer engagement with these actions?*

CONCEPTS IN DEPTH The tools in this section apply the concepts discussed at length in the book, *From the Top Down: The Executive Role in Successful Volunteer Involvement, 3rd edition,* by Susan J. Ellis (Philadelphia: Energize, Inc., 2010), specifically:
- Chapter 5: Understanding the Volunteer-Employee Relationship
- Chapter 6: Strategies to Create Teamwork

Introduction to the Executive Role

It is common to talk about the need for organizations to provide volunteer-friendly organizations—the type of environment that provides a welcoming and supportive place for volunteers to contribute their service. While this is clearly important, many organizations fail to realize that it is equally crucial to support paid staff in effectively partnering with volunteers.

The executive director, in guiding the culture for volunteer engagement, must make certain that staff expectations and accountability are clear, and that all staff—from clerical to managerial levels—feel genuinely committed to volunteer success. Also, staff must be equipped with training that increases their competency in partnering with volunteers, and they must be rewarded for working with volunteers effectively.

Therefore, this section provides tools for executives to assess staff commitment to involving volunteers and to be involved in promoting the four key foundations for commitment to volunteer engagement:

- Clarity of expectations

- Competency to do the job

- Involvement and influence in the planning

- Appreciation for excellence in partnering effectively with volunteers

Hiring or appointing a knowledgeable, experienced director of volunteer involvement will go a long way toward creating a positive environment, but it's the executive who must ensure that the organization is as staff-friendly as it is volunteer-friendly. True partnership between volunteers and employees depends on satisfying both groups of workers, not forcing the paid staff to accommodate volunteer needs at the expense of staff needs.

Several of the tools in this section are adaptations of worksheets I included in my introduction to *Training Busy Staff to Succeed with Volunteers: The 55-Minute Training Series* (Stallings 2007). If you ask staff to complete these forms, make sure that the request is made jointly by the director of volunteer involvement and the executive director. This adds strength to the request, validates the process, and makes it clear that staff should cooperate fully.

"True partnership between volunteers and employees depends on satisfying both groups of workers..."

Executive Perspective on Strengthening Staff Partnerships with Volunteers

As executive, what is your point of view on the following issues critical to assuring full staff commitment and competency in partnering with volunteers? Consider each question on your own and/or with your senior management team.

1. Do you think that training in volunteer management principles is important to get staff ready to partner effectively with volunteers?

2. Do you know who on staff now is a great supervisor of volunteers? Do you know who needs improvement at or resists working with volunteers? What actions could you take in light of such assessments?

3. What is the attitude of senior managers and middle managers about volunteer engagement? How knowledgeable are these administrators about what to expect from staff in their departments in partnering with volunteers? How knowledgeable are they about their role in supporting this teamwork?

4. When hiring new staff, do you consider applicants' experience, motivation, and skills in working with volunteers?

5. Do you think that the role of staff in supervising volunteers is clearly defined? If yes, how is this expectation conveyed? How could it be improved?

6. Are staff evaluated on their work with volunteers? If yes, how is this accomplished? How could it be improved?

7. In what ways are staff rewarded for excellence in working with volunteers? If none, what ways could they be rewarded?

8. Currently, what orientation and training is given to new staff about working with volunteers? Is this effective and sufficient? Is there periodic in-service training to refresh and update knowledge on this subject?

9. How do you keep informed about trends and issues in volunteerism? Does anyone attend professional conferences about volunteering, read publications in the field, follow online resources, etc.?

10. What is a realistic expectation of the level of support for staff training in working with volunteers, particularly in terms of allocating time and resources to preparing, producing, and attending training?

Survey: Assessing Staff Commitment to Partner with Volunteers

Purpose:

This is a self-assessment tool, based on *Coaching for Commitment: Interpersonal Strategies for Obtaining Superior Performance* by Dennis C. Kinlaw (Kinlaw, 1999), to identify potential reasons for staff resistance to engaging volunteers.

Discussion Ideas:

- Note that the grid has four sections: clarity, competency, influence, and appreciation. Discuss how these are the cornerstones of building commitment.

- Talk about any surprises in the collective responses.

- Spend time on those items that most respondents checked as "no" or "partially," as these are most likely the root of any staff resistance.

- Discuss how the issues identified can be improved or changed.

- Consider how such changes would increase staff commitment to volunteer engagement.

- Discuss methods to address the identified issues and assign action steps to appropriate staff (including executives) to diminish negative issues raised.

Process:

Option 1

- Ask paid staff, including yourself and other top managers, to fill out this form based on their personal perspective, and return it to you by a set date.

- Tally the responses without identifying anyone individually.

- Then call a meeting, give out the summary of responses, and discuss (see below). (Large organizations can conduct the survey and discussions with staff in each unit or department.)

Option 2

If you believe that staff will feel safe in discussing their concerns and problems publicly:

- Convene staff, including yourself and other top managers, and give people time to fill out this form individually.

- Then discuss their responses as a group.

Option 3

If you believe that staff will resist discussing their concerns and problems publicly:

- Convene staff, including yourself and other top managers, and give people time to fill out this form individually.

- Collect and redistribute the forms so that no one knows whose form they have. By calling out the responses, tally them as a group.

- Then discuss the aggregate results.

Assessing Staff Commitment
to Partner with Volunteers

Clarity	Yes	Partially	No	Need to Learn More
1. Do you understand what is expected of you concerning the supervision of volunteers in our organization?				
2. Are your responsibilities concerning volunteers outlined in your job description?				
3. Were you told the purpose and philosophy of volunteer involvement at staff orientation or another appropriate time?				
4. Are you evaluated on how effective you are in working with volunteers in your performance appraisals and consideration for promotion?				
Competence/Support				
1. Do you have experience being a volunteer and/or partnering with volunteers elsewhere that you can apply to working with volunteers here?				
2. Do you understand basic theories and the skills of volunteer supervision?				
3. Do you have the necessary skills to partner successfully with volunteers?				
4. Is training in volunteer supervision currently available to you?				
5. Do you have enough time to support volunteers in their work?				
6. Do you have whatever space, supplies, materials, or resources needed for volunteers to do the work in your unit?				

(continued)

Assessing Staff Commitment to Partner with Volunteers
(continued)

Influence	Yes	Partially	No	Need to Learn More
1. Have you been involved in planning of the volunteer opportunities offered?				
2. Do you have final say in the selection of volunteers who will report to you?				
3. Is there encouragement for innovation and creativity in implementing volunteer activities?				
4. Are you asked for feedback on volunteer performance and projects as they evolve?				
5. Are you involved in evaluating volunteer work?				
Appreciation				
1. Are you formally recognized for outstanding work with volunteers?				
2. Are you informally recognized for your ongoing support of volunteers and the volunteer office?				
3. When volunteers are recognized, are staff partners also acknowledged?				

How Executives Ensure that All Staff Are Clear on What Is Expected from Them in Working with Volunteers

☐ Develop written policies and procedures that outline your organization's standard volunteer management practices, both expectations of staff in partnering with volunteers and expectations of volunteers in doing their work.

☐ Ensure that the job descriptions of all employees include the responsibility of working successfully with volunteers.

☐ Ask questions of job applicants about past experience or training in working with volunteers (which is different than asking about what the person him or herself has done *as* a volunteer).

☐ Add information about how employees are expected to partner with volunteers (and work with the volunteer involvement staff) in all new staff orientation, the employee handbook, and other appropriate materials.

☐ Ensure that employees are evaluated on their ability to work with volunteers in annual performance reviews—and are recognized for success or asked to improve if they fall short.

☐ Schedule time to discuss volunteer-related topics in staff meetings.

☐ Provide training on working with volunteers to both new staff and as continuing professional education.

☐ Ask questions about how volunteers are being engaged in each unit's activities and request that this information be included in unit reports (apart from what is in the report submitted by volunteer involvement staff on organization-wide volunteer contributions).

☐ Include mention of the importance of and goals for volunteer engagement in all organization documents and public materials.

☐ Develop a one-page summary of the tasks an employee will be expected to perform in partnering with volunteers. (*see next page*)

☐ Make certain that all staff are clear on the role of the person designated to lead volunteer involvement.

Staff Actions in Partnering with Volunteers

For all staff to feel comfortable and be effective in partnering with volunteers, they must first have a clear understanding of what is expected of them in this role: **clarity of expectations.** They also deserve the opportunity to give input as to what their role is going to be on a daily basis: **involvement and influence in the planning.** This is an important step in developing their **competency to do the job,** since one must know *what* to do in order to do it well.

Consider developing a guide summarizing the various stages of welcoming, working with, and saying good-bye to volunteers, and identifying specific activities that a paid staff member would need to do at each stage. See the example on the next page, which presents some generic activities often expected. When you create this guide for your organization, of course, you can include the most likely scenarios for your setting. Here's how:

1. Form a task force including managers, the director of volunteer involvement, line staff, and representative volunteers to discuss what a staff member needs to do over the course of a volunteer's time in the organization to assure success.

2. From this discussion, write a summary of your organization's expectations when staff partner with volunteers.

3. To add clout to the summary, sign it to show it is endorsed by the executive.

Once developed, this guide has many possible uses:

- Give to new staff during their orientation or as the director of volunteer involvement introduces the new hire to how volunteers participate in your organization

- Update and redistribute annually during a staff meeting or a retreat focused on volunteer engagement

- Use as a tool by a supervisor to review staff compliance and effectiveness in partnering with volunteers

See example on next page.

Staff Actions in Partnering with Volunteers

Any staff who partner with volunteers in carrying out our mission are expected to perform the following activities:

1. **Interview prospective volunteers**

    All individuals interested in volunteering with you should be interviewed by you to determine if they are a good match for your position.

2. **Provide Orientation and Training**

    This should be done to ensure that the volunteer is sufficiently prepared for the work they have agreed to perform.

3. **One-Month Evaluation**

    Establish a convenient time, approximately one month after volunteer starts, for a mutual performance appraisal/conversation.. The focal point of this discussion is a review and update of the volunteer's position description and the agreement form signed by both parties at the initial interview. Suggest any adjustments and changes to improve the working relationship. If the volunteer is not able to keep his or her commitments or perform the assigned tasks, refer her or him back to the director of volunteer involvement for possible placement into a different position.

4. **Ongoing Support**

    Your goal is to provide resources, guidance, and feedback to enable the volunteer to be successful in his or her work. This should be done in a timely, supportive fashion.

5. **Recordkeeping**

    Remind the volunteer of the importance of keeping monthly time and activity records, and assess the impact of the efforts of all volunteers for insurance purposes.

6. **Ongoing Recognition**

    The organization's annual recognition event is a formal acknowledgment of volunteers but it should always be supplemented by your personal, spontaneous acts of appreciation at the time good work is done.

(continued)

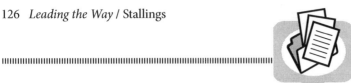

Staff Actions in Partnering with Volunteers
(continued)

7. **Exit Interviews When Volunteers Leave**

   When a volunteer leaves his or her position it is helpful to have a face-to-face or telephone exit interview to discuss why they are leaving and to thank the volunteer for service up to that point. If this is not possible, ask the volunteer to fill out an exit survey form (can be by e-mail) and return it to the Volunteer Resources Office. The purpose of gathering this information is to provide feedback and guidance to strengthen our volunteer program.

8. **Dealing with Unsatisfactory Performance**

   If a volunteer is not performing well after expectations have been made clear and supervisory coaching provided, it may be necessary to request that she or he be transferred to another position or released entirely from being a volunteer in the organization. In these rare situations, contact the Volunteer Involvement Office for any necessary support or assistance.

_____   _____

Executive Director   **Director of Volunteer Involvement**

Building Staff Competence through Training

Often executives endorse training for staff but then exempt managers from attending. If volunteers are to be integrated throughout the organization, senior staff should participate in the planning and training as well. Although the actual responsibility of training may be designated to the director of volunteer involvement, it is important for the executive to be aware of potential training topics and to encourage all staff to receive sufficient training/coaching to partner effectively with volunteers.

Planning for Staff Training

- Survey and communicate with staff about training topics that will meet their needs in working with volunteers.

- Involve appropriate paid and volunteer staff in planning and delivering training.

- Ensure the training is fun, efficient, and practical.

- Join with other volunteer-involving organizations in your community to share costs in presenting training.

- Evaluate training to determine its impact and to get input for future topics.

Potential Topics to Include in Staff Training

- Creating assignments that will attract volunteers

- Interviewing volunteers

- Understanding and responding to different volunteer motivations (why do people volunteer?)

- Trends in volunteering and which trends are having an impact on your organization

- Dos and don'ts of supervising and partnering with volunteers

- Designing and updating training for volunteers

- Delegating while maintaining ultimate responsibility

- Mutual performance reviews of staff/volunteer partnerships

- When volunteers don't perform…

(continued)

Building Staff Competence through Training
(continued)

- Evaluating volunteer performance

- Showing appreciation to volunteers

- Building commitment to volunteer engagement: What's the possible return on investment?

- Recruiting messages that speak to different generations

- Understanding and managing a multi-generation volunteer force (volunteer style differences among Baby Boomers, Generation X, and Millennials)

- Why volunteers leave; tips on retention

- Integrating volunteers into an organization's or department's culture

- How to engage short-term and episodic volunteers

- How to engage highly skilled and pro bono volunteers

- How to design group volunteer projects

- How to deal with difficult volunteer situations

- When volunteers "age in place"…

- Time management in working with volunteers

- Firing a volunteer

- The similarities and differences in supervising volunteers and paid staff

- The organizational support needed to ensure volunteer success

INSTRUCTIONS FOR

Survey: Determining Staff Training Needs for Working with Volunteers

Purpose:

Another cornerstone of commitment is **influence and involvement.**

The following survey is meant to be distributed to staff members to get their input on the content and design of training in how to partner with volunteers. While the responses will provide important guidance to curriculum development, there are other reasons this form is important:

- The questions are thought-provokers in themselves and should make staff stop and think about volunteer engagement.

- Doing the needs assessment sends the signal that working effectively with volunteers is a key expectation of all staff and that training will be provided to assure everyone has the skills to do this.

- By inviting staff to give their opinions, they will feel that they are involved in the organization's volunteer engagement rather than simply carrying out a role imparted to them.

- By having both the director of volunteer involvement and the executive director sign the message at the top, the activity is clearly supported by top management and thus has credence.

Process:

As executive, assist in the development of the questions or review the questionnaire prior to its being given to all staff.

- Take note of the introductory statement at the top of the survey. It is meant to be co-signed by the executive director and leader of volunteer engagement to emphasize the importance of completing the survey.

- Distribute the form to staff, either during a meeting or individually.

- Review the summary of results provided by the director of volunteer involvement or person carrying out the questionnaire and respond with thoughts/ recommendations.

- Be sure to report the collective results to everyone as soon as possible to affirm that someone read and intends to use the responses.

- Develop training in working with volunteers as needed.

Determining Staff Training Needs
for Working with Volunteers

This survey is part of the organization's plan to enhance our delivery of services to our clients. The information you share will assist in the design of in-service training for staff and leadership volunteers who work directly with volunteers to carry out our mission. Your thoughtful and honest responses will allow us to design the training to address your concerns and issues as much as possible. The individual information will be kept confidential but collective themes and recommendations will be utilized in proposing training topics and methods. Thank you!

_____   _____
Director of Volunteer Involvement Signature   Executive Director Signature

Circle the number showing your response from Strongly Disagree (1) to Strongly Agree (5).					
1. The time and effort I invest in supervising volunteers is well worth it because of the benefits accrued from volunteer service.	1	2	3	4	5
2. Volunteer participation enables me to perform activities/tasks I would not otherwise be able to do.	1	2	3	4	5
3. Volunteers are oriented toward an understanding of my priorities, concerns, frustrations, etc., as a staff person.	1	2	3	4	5
4. In general, volunteers I have worked with are qualified for their positions in our organization.	1	2	3	4	5
5. I feel recognized and rewarded for my efforts with volunteers.	1	2	3	4	5
6. I would feel more competent in my involvement with volunteers if I had: a. more information about our volunteer engagement strategy	1	2	3	4	5
b. greater clarity about my role as a supervisor of volunteers	1	2	3	4	5
c. training in the skills of supervising or partnering with volunteers	1	2	3	4	5
d. more involvement in planning/evaluation of volunteer opportunities/initiatives	1	2	3	4	5

(continued)

Determining Staff Training Needs
for Working with Volunteers
(continued)

Circle the number showing your response from No Interest/Need (1) to Strong Interest/Need (5).					
7. Rate your interest or need in gaining these skills in partnering with volunteers: a. Interviewing	1	2	3	4	5
b. Supervising	1	2	3	4	5
c. Recruiting volunteers	1	2	3	4	5
d. Supervising and coaching	1	2	3	4	5
e. Orienting volunteers new to the organization or volunteers with new roles	1	2	3	4	5
f. Motivating volunteers	1	2	3	4	5
g. Recognizing volunteers for their work and showing them appreciation	1	2	3	4	5
h. Evaluating the work of volunteers and providing them feedback	1	2	3	4	5
i. Delegating work to volunteers	1	2	3	4	5
j. Training/coaching volunteers	1	2	3	4	5
k. Managing risk related to volunteer activities	1	2	3	4	5
l. Dealing with difficult behavior of volunteers	1	2	3	4	5
m. Other topics: _____	1	2	3	4	5

(continued)

Determining Staff Training Needs
for Working with Volunteers
(continued)

8. What do you see as the major problems or barriers to involving volunteers more effectively in our organization?

    _____

    _____

    _____

    _____

9. Please elaborate on any specific concerns/requests that you would like to see addressed in volunteer management training for staff and volunteer leaders in our organization.

    _____

    _____

    _____

    _____

(Optional)

Name_____

Position_____

Ways to Show Appreciation for
Staff Excellence in Partnering with Volunteers

Executives can and should be involved in setting the tone for appreciating staff who are successful in partnering with volunteers. An executive who is involved with any of these techniques is showing the value she or he places on effective volunteer engagement.

- During any formal recognition, recognize the staff member who works with each group of volunteers. This team recognition acknowledges the work of staff, too. It also reinforces the philosophy that volunteers and staff work as partners in carrying out the mission of the organization.

- Highlight excellence in staff engagement of volunteers when the employee has:

  - Created particularly creative and new types of volunteer positions

  - Done an outstanding job in delegating to and supporting volunteers

  - Created an innovative volunteer training program

  - Introduced new ways to recognize and thank volunteers

  - Done an excellent job of creating and supporting a group project

  - Been a role model for other staff less experienced or committed to working with volunteers

  - Demonstrated new ways to gain volunteer input

  - Served on a task force or volunteer management team to strengthen overall volunteer involvement

  - Recruited friends/family/acquaintances to serve as volunteers in the organization

  - Participated as a presenter in staff skills training for effective volunteer engagement

  - Made an outstanding presentation to the board about the impact of volunteers on the mission

- Note excellence in volunteer engagement in the staff member's personnel file and in any annual or other staff reviews/evaluation.

- Ask staff for input in designing and evaluating volunteer participation.

(continued)

Ways to Show Appreciation for
Staff Excellence in Partnering with Volunteers
(continued)

- Feature the staff's work with volunteers in information sent to the board or to any other organizational stakeholders.

- Highlight staff excellence in partnering with volunteers in reports to funders.

- Informally acknowledge a staff person's support of volunteers by thanking them personally, in conversation or with a note. Or give noticeable recognition in the form of an item/trinket that acknowledges appreciation for their team work and leadership in working with volunteers.

- Ask volunteers for nominations of the "Staff Person Who Most Supported Our Efforts at Volunteering" and present that award at a recognition event.

- Share examples of staff support of volunteers via any electronic means available (Web site, e-mail, blogs, etc.).

- At a recognition event, have volunteers share their appreciation for staff in some manner: formal, informal, serious, humorous.

EXECUTIVE SELF-ASSESSMENT

Do I ensure staff commitment and competence in volunteer engagement with these actions?

1. I promote our philosophy of the value of volunteer engagement throughout the organization.

   ☐ Yes ☐ No ☐ Sometimes ☐ Will now initiate ☐ Not relevant

2. I endorse the policy of hiring staff who have a positive philosophy about volunteers and experience in partnering with volunteers.

   ☐ Yes ☐ No ☐ Sometimes ☐ Will now initiate ☐ Not relevant

3. I require staff job descriptions that clearly articulate the responsibility for working or partnering with volunteers.

   ☐ Yes ☐ No ☐ Sometimes ☐ Will now initiate ☐ Not relevant

4. I endorse evaluating job performance in the area of partnering with volunteers.

   ☐ Yes ☐ No ☐ Sometimes ☐ Will now initiate ☐ Not relevant

5. I expect staff to participate in orienting, training, and supervising volunteers.

   ☐ Yes ☐ No ☐ Sometimes ☐ Will now initiate ☐ Not relevant

6. I provide opportunities for staff to give honest feedback about their experiences with volunteers.

   ☐ Yes ☐ No ☐ Sometimes ☐ Will now initiate ☐ Not relevant

7. I attempt to diminish barriers to staff working effectively with volunteers.

   ☐ Yes ☐ No ☐ Sometimes ☐ Will now initiate ☐ Not relevant

8. I support mutual evaluation sessions between staff and volunteers to applaud successes and identify any needed changes.

   ☐ Yes ☐ No ☐ Sometimes ☐ Will now initiate ☐ Not relevant

(continued)

Do I ensure staff commitment and competence in volunteer engagement with these actions?

(continued)

9. I provide or give access to relevant skills training for all staff who are expected to work with volunteers at any level.

   ☐ Yes   ☐ No   ☐ Sometimes   ☐ Will now initiate   ☐ Not relevant

10. I encourage and participate in recognizing and showing appreciation for staff who successfully partner with volunteers.

    ☐ Yes   ☐ No   ☐ Sometimes   ☐ Will now initiate   ☐ Not relevant

11. I acknowledge and allow for the time and resource investment it takes to partner with volunteers effectively.

    ☐ Yes   ☐ No   ☐ Sometimes   ☐ Will now initiate   ☐ Not relevant

Integrating Volunteers throughout the Organization

*T*he volunteer program is fully integrated into the life of the agency.
*The coordinator works collaboratively with other
managers/programs to strengthen fund development, public affairs, education and other service
areas. Managers now see the coordinator and the
volunteers as essential resources that help them
accomplish their goals more effectively. A major
challenge was breaking down the silos of work.*

David Greenberg, President and CEO
Planned Parenthood
of the Columbia/Willamette Chapter
Portland, Oregon

---

*The role of the volunteer is integral to our orga-
nization and I definitely make that known to the
team. Leadership comes from the top and when
the leaders act as a positive role model in working
with volunteers, the team will follow. One must
walk the talk.*

Suzanne Jackett, CEO,
Between Friends Club
- recreation for people with disabilities
Calgary, Alberta, Canada

**CONCEPTS
IN DEPTH**

The tools in this section apply the concepts discussed at length in the book,
*From the Top Down: The Executive Role
in Successful Volunteer Involvement, 3rd
edition,* by Susan J. Ellis (Philadelphia:
Energize, Inc., 2010), specifically:

- Chapter 2: Considerations in Planning
- Chapter 4: Staffing Volunteer Involvement
- Chapter 6: Strategies to Create Teamwork
- Chapter 7: Tapping into the Full Spectrum
  of Volunteer Resources

CONTENTS

||||||||||||||||||||||||||||||||||||||||||||||||||||||||||||||||||||||||||||||||||||||||||||||||||||||||||||||||||||||||||||||||||||||||||||||||

Introduction to the Executive Role

The best volunteer engagement efforts put no limits on the variety of ways skilled and willing community members can contribute to the work of an organization. This means actively deploying volunteers into all departments and projects, at any level from frontline services to executive administration. The result is a blending of the work of paid and unpaid staff in a seamless and collaborative way that extends the reach of the organization beyond what it could have done without volunteers.

If your organization has not moved beyond the traditional ways of engaging volunteers (commonly as helpers or fundraisers on the sidelines of the organization's integral work), consider expanding your idea of what the right volunteers might do for the organization. Don't miss out on the full range of volunteer talent!

An element essential to integrating volunteers is maximizing the coordination and mutual support between staff from each department and the person designated to lead your organization's volunteer involvement initiative (to whom we refer as "director of volunteer involvement"). As Susan Ellis notes in her book *From the Top Down,* "It takes a village to raise a child and it takes the entire organization to support volunteers" (Ellis 2010). No matter how fantastic she or he is, the director of volunteer involvement cannot single-handedly achieve full integration and acceptance of volunteer work. The executive must promote collaborative interaction between the leader of volunteer resources and all those who carry out specific functions in the organization such as marketing, information technology, fundraising, and more.

The following tools will guide you as you encourage each department head or designated staff member(s) to consider the interrelationship of their work and volunteer involvement.

1. The first Idea Stimulator, "Integrating Volunteers throughout the Organization," offers an overview of how volunteer engagement benefits the entire organization and should be interrelated with each function, department, or work area. The chart shows:

   • What each area of an organization can gain from the efforts of the right volunteers; and

   • The impact of intentional collaboration between the staff of that area and the director of volunteer involvement.

2. The second Idea Stimulator, "Mutual Expectations between the Volunteer Involvement Staff and All Staff/Departments Partnering with Volunteers," outlines the way any department head or unit supervisor should expect to work together with the director of volunteer involvement on a continuous basis. As executive, you can ensure that such cooperation and collaboration happens. This Mutual Expectations sheet can be used along with all of the specific "Collaboration Strategies" that follow.

3. Then you'll find eleven detailed Collaboration Strategy guidelines for how to make the benefits of volunteer involvement real, department by department—how each function should integrate their work with the volunteer office so as to support each other, avoid duplication of effort, maximize each department's skills and expertise, and do what is best for successful volunteer participation. These are meant to open discussion. Your staff will of course want to add other points relevant to your setting and their units.

4. After the Collaboration Strategy sheets there's "A Guide to Expanding Volunteer Engagement," which is a set of questions to elicit creative thinking about potential new volunteer position opportunities. Whether this worksheet is used by an executive, a unit manager, or the director of volunteer involvement, the process of developing roles for volunteers is applicable to any department.

5. Finally, to practice what you preach, there's a "Starter Set of Ideas for Volunteer Talent to Support *You*—the Executive!"

> *"An element essential to integrating volunteers is maximizing the coordination and mutual support between staff from each department and the person designated to lead your organization's volunteer involvement initiative."*

Integrating Volunteers throughout the Organization

Board of Directors or Other Governing Authority

The board of directors (volunteers themselves) must be involved in articulating a vision and long-range planning for volunteer engagement, approve the allocation of resources to support volunteers, and review progress regularly. The director of volunteer involvement is the in-house expert on trends and issues in volunteerism and therefore serves as a consultant to the board in the planning process and can assist with recruitment of new board and committee members as well.

What Qualified Volunteers Can Contribute to Governance:

- Serve as nonprofit board members
- Bring a wide range of expertise and community perspectives to service on board sub-committees and task forces
- Attend a board meeting to educate the board on special topics
- Serve on a volunteerism advisory council along with paid staff, board members, and executives

Executive Leadership and Administration

Effective volunteer involvement carries out the organization's mission and brings in financial and in-kind resources. Volunteers are the non-paid staff of the organization (often outnumbering the employees) and need and deserve executive attention. The leader of volunteer efforts needs active executive support to ensure success of volunteer engagement because many of these actions require organization-wide, interdepartmental authority. Further, when CEOs and other top administrators involve volunteers in their own work, they send a message to all staff that volunteers are valued and integral to all parts of the organization.

By communicating with the CEO regularly, the director of volunteer involvement can ensure that the CEO is informed about volunteer involvement and has the knowledge to consider volunteer involvement when making organizational strategies.

What Qualified Volunteers Can Contribute to Executive Staff:

- Access to new professional and business contacts, financial donors, and in-kind resources

(continued)

Integrating Volunteers
throughout the Organization

(continued)

- Consulting, advising, and support services ranging from research studies to speech writing to investment strategies

Programs and Services for the Organization's Clients

Programs and services for clients are the core function of the organization—all other departments exist to enable these services to happen. Therefore, the majority of volunteers will be recruited to help deliver these programs, either in direct service or in supportive, administrative, or clerical roles. The volunteer involvement staff must therefore work closely with program managers and frontline staff to:

- Design and update volunteer positions

- Recruit and place the most qualified volunteers

- Make certain that employees are trained to partner effectively with today's volunteers

- Make sure that volunteers are trained in how to team up with paid staff

What Qualified Volunteers Can Contribute to Programs and Services:

Helping to provide direct service to those the organization serves—be they clients, audience members, patients, residents, or the general public—is what most volunteers are recruited to do. In many organizations volunteers far outnumber paid staff and perform all core service delivery, with employees coordinating their efforts. In other situations, volunteers augment the work of paid staff, giving individualized attention to clients, doing extra things that employees do not have time to do, or helping client families. What a qualified and willing volunteer can do is limited only by the creativity of the organization in seeking such help.

Development, Fundraising, Special Events

The cross-over between volunteers and donors is (or could be) significant, so these offices are potentially dealing with the same people. Volunteers are the leaders and backbone of all kinds of large and targeted special events, but should be integrated administratively with all other volunteers helping the organization. Since volunteers are often an organization's biggest supporters, volunteers

(continued)

Integrating Volunteers throughout the Organization

(continued)

may become donors when invited properly. Conversely, donors may respond positively to invitations to volunteer. Fundraising staff and volunteer involvement staff are both out in the community making friends for the organization, so their messages about giving of money and donating time should be integrated and consistent.

What Qualified Volunteers Can Contribute to Fundraising and Development:

- Donate or generate funds

- Initiate or follow up contacts with new or lapsed donors—and can do so as supporters of the organization who themselves get no financial benefit from any money raised

- Use their wide circle of contacts (often quite different from those of paid staff) to open new doors to money, in-kind donations, and new volunteers

Public Relations, Community Outreach, Marketing, Web Site and Social Media

All public and community relations outreach should incorporate some invitation to volunteer, just as all volunteer recruitment messages should convey a positive image of the organization. Committed volunteers are an organization's best public relations agents and can be asked to serve as spokespeople to their circle of contacts, as well as represent the community's point of view back to the agency.

Today, the public relations function also includes managing the organization's Web site, on which volunteer involvement must have a presence to demonstrate their importance to the organization, provide recognition to current volunteers, and recruit new ones. Current volunteer opportunities should be posted and updated, and an online application process developed. The volunteer involvement staff can provide information/stories/pictures for the Web site and volunteers to advise on and monitor social media.

What Qualified Volunteers Can Contribute to Public Relations:

- Open additional circles of acquaintances and contacts that may be resources to the organization or candidates to receive services from the organization

(continued)

Integrating Volunteers throughout the Organization

(continued)

- Serve on a speakers bureau
- Conduct surveys in the community to identify needs or assess public attitudes
- Represent the organization at community events
- Provide a continuous flow of updated information for social media sites
- Help design Web pages and maintain content
- Moderate blogs and monitor Web postings from site visitors

Personnel, Human Resources, Staff Education

Volunteers are the organization's unpaid staff. This means that personnel policies for employees should be expanded to cover volunteers, as well as provide direction to employees in partnering with volunteers. Responsibility for working with volunteers needs to be stated in employee job descriptions. Together, the human resources and volunteer involvement staff can offer training to employees in volunteer supervision, delegation, and communication skills.

What Qualified Volunteers Can Contribute to Human Resources:

- Design and conduct satisfaction surveys of employees, clients, volunteers, or the community at large
- Research evolving labor law and related issues
- Advise on personnel policies
- Help to find the best job applicants
- For staff and/or volunteer training needs, experts can be found in any subject who can share their knowledge in presentations

Information Technology

Information technology (IT) staff support volunteers just as they support employees: providing password access to intranets or databases, designating e-mail addresses, training in special software, and more. While the public relations staff develops the content for the organization's Web site, the IT staff is often responsible for timely posting of material, creating online forms such as volunteer applications, and other online tools needed by volunteer involvement staff.

(continued)

Integrating Volunteers
throughout the Organization
(continued)

What Qualified Volunteers Can Contribute to Information Technology:

- Help IT staff to stay on top of the rapid changes and new products in this field

- Pro bono consulting on decisions about what software, networks, or data management systems would best meet the organization's needs

- Quality assurance testers to do trial runs of software or database applications after changes have been made by IT personnel

- Depending on experience with Web design software, can post approved content to the Web site

- Proofread Web postings and check for broken links

- Monitor e-mails from the Web site

Advocacy, Public Education, Government Relations

Many volunteers are proponents of organizational causes and, if organized, can lead or greatly supplement advocacy to elected officials and others who have the power and influence to impact the cause. Staff who deal with public education/advocacy can provide all volunteers pertinent information that they, in turn, can share within their circles of influence. Volunteers, as private citizens, can write to their elected officials to urge critical votes.

What Qualified Volunteers Can Contribute to Advocacy:

- In smaller organizations, there may not be any staff person whose full-time responsibility is advocacy and public education, making this an ideal area for volunteer involvement

- Can use their connection with the larger community to spearhead the effort on advocacy issues

- Carry out public education campaigns in specific geographic areas or with designated target populations

- As concerned private citizens, can contact legislators to urge action and votes

(continued)

Integrating Volunteers
throughout the Organization
(continued)

Accounting, Finance

Expert volunteers can assist with internal control, informal auditing, and investment decisions. The accounting staff can ensure that volunteer-run events handle cash and sales properly. The volunteer treasurer of the board is the conduit of financial information to the board of directors, who, in turn, oversee the organization's financial activity.

What Qualified Volunteers Can Contribute to Finance:

- Be investment/financial systems coaches
- Interpret financial data and forecast financial futures

Legal Compliance and Risk Management

As part of the organization's workforce, volunteers must perform their work legally and safely and, in turn, be protected for their own safety and defense from liability. Working together, the legal and volunteer involvement staff can develop necessary forms such as waivers or parental permission slips, do a risk assessment of new volunteer positions, and provide risk management training.

What Qualified Volunteers Can Contribute to Legal Compliance and Risk Management:

- Be pro bono consultants to organizations without on-site legal staff
- Develop and review policies
- Assess risk potential
- Advise on any necessary legal compliance issues, including accessibility for people with disabilities

Maintenance/Security/Physical Plant

Because of the way volunteer involvement activities occur, the maintenance staff provides support by keeping the organization's facility open odd hours, setting up furniture for group meetings, and generally keeping the offices attractive and safe for volunteers and staff. Volunteers can identify repair needs or potential hazards that need to be addressed for the health of clients and visitors. Individual and group volunteers recruited by volunteer staff can provide additional hands for clean-up, building, or beautification projects for the organization's facility.

(continued)

Integrating Volunteers
throughout the Organization
(continued)

What Qualified Volunteers Can Contribute to Maintenance of the Physical Plant:

- Apply their trade and crafts skills to anything from building playgrounds to landscaping

- Community gardeners can assist in beautifying a site and in planting a food-producing garden

- Maintain the grounds or do behind-the-scenes preparation and clean-up for large events

- Organize and participate in a group clean-up or beautification project

Mutual Expectations between the Volunteer Involvement Staff and All Staff/Departments Partnering with Volunteers

To do what is best for volunteers, the director of volunteer involvement must function in ways that are not typical for other department heads. Because volunteers might be placed in any unit or program in the organization, and might work with staff at any level of authority, the person responsible for volunteer engagement (here called "director of volunteer involvement") also needs to interact with everyone. To ensure collaboration, all participants need to understand their own roles as well as that of the director of volunteer involvement. Here are some basic expectations to clarify role expectations and to hold each other accountable:

Paid staff can expect the director of volunteer involvement to:

- Be knowledgeable about trends and issues in volunteering and skilled in best volunteer management practices.

- Be aware of the work done in each area so as to help in creating volunteer position descriptions.

- Be accountable for recruiting qualified volunteers from which staff can select the best suited for their available positions.

- Act as a consultant in crafting work for volunteers that is do-able, meaningful, manageable by staff, and attractive to volunteers.

- Act as a third-party support to both staff and volunteers in any disputes.

- Advocate for volunteers and, when they are not present to speak for themselves, represent their voice and potential when necessary.

- Offer training and resources to make certain that staff have the skills to partner effectively with volunteers.

The director of volunteer involvement can expect individual staff who partner with volunteers to:

- Identify meaningful roles the right volunteers can fill in their area of work.

- Ensure that any person wishing to volunteer—whether a friend, donor, student intern, or someone else known to the department—registers officially with the volunteer office.

(continued)

Mutual Expectations between the Volunteer Involvement Staff and All Staff/Departments Partnering with Volunteers

(continued)

- Keep the volunteer office informed of any changes in a volunteer's participation.

- Keep records and submit reports as requested on volunteers assigned to them.

- Be welcoming and appreciative of volunteers, while also holding them accountable for their work.

- Orient volunteers to their worksite and give appropriate training to carry out the work.

- Provide ongoing support and resources to volunteers who work with them.

- Involve/inform the volunteer office if there is a significant problem/issue involving volunteers that needs special attention from the director of volunteer involvement.

In a larger organization, a department head or unit supervisor should also:

- Allow staff the time to supervise volunteers assigned to them.

- Designate someone to be the point of contact between the unit and the volunteer office, to ensure efficient communication.

- Be open to a variety of volunteers, each of whom may bring something unique to the department. Involve the director of volunteer involvement at the planning stage of new projects, rather than after-the-fact to "produce volunteers."

- Provide information to evaluate the effectiveness and impact of volunteers working in their area.

Volunteer Involvement
and the Board of Directors

The board must pay attention to and ask questions about volunteer contributions, which reinforces the organization's commitment to these supporters. The leader of volunteer involvement has unique expertise on trends and issues in volunteerism which governing officials can tap into for their long-range planning for volunteer engagement and also in recruiting the best board member volunteers.

> *Here are ways the board and volunteer involvement staff can maximize each other's skills and expertise, and do what is best for successful volunteer involvement.*

- The board inquires about what roles volunteers will play in any new proposed project, program, or initiative.

- The director of volunteer involvement gives regular presentations to keep board members current on trends and issues in volunteerism.

- The board of directors allocates needed funds in the organization's budget to support volunteer involvement.

- The board asks for and examines regular reports on volunteer involvement.

- The director of volunteer involvement prepares and presents those reports to the board.

- Board members give the director of volunteer involvement access to their business and professional contacts for recruitment purposes, either by introduction to the right contact person or through personal endorsement. Examples of helpful actions include:

  - Keeping their business employees and colleagues informed about volunteer opportunities in the agency, through in-house publications or intranet postings.

  - Inviting the director of volunteer involvement to exhibit or speak about volunteer needs.

  - Making personal referrals of prospective volunteers with specific skills to the director of volunteer involvement.

(continued)

Volunteer Involvement Staff and the Board of Directors
(continued)

- The director of volunteer involvement is involved in orienting and training new board or advisory council members.

- They combine efforts to recruit new board and committee volunteers.

- Board members attend formal volunteer recognition events and interact with direct service volunteers.

- Board members participate in new volunteer orientation sessions.

- Board members spend some time as a frontline volunteer to gain firsthand knowledge of the organization's work (understanding that this means doing whatever tasks are assigned while in this role and not expecting special treatment as a board member).

Also see section eight for more on the role of the board of directors in volunteer involvement.

Volunteer Involvement
and Senior Executives/Administrators

The leader of volunteer involvement needs active executive support to ensure success of volunteer engagement because many of his or her efforts require organization-wide, interdepartmental authority. Conversely, there are many ways executives can make use of the director of volunteer involvement's expertise in volunteerism.

> *The following are ways these leaders should integrate their work so as to support each other, avoid duplication of effort, maximize each other's skills and expertise, and do what is best for successful volunteer involvement.*

- Administrators include discussion of volunteers—how they might contribute and how they might be affected—in any strategic planning.

- The director of volunteer involvement either serves on the senior management team or is invited to participate whenever any planning is being discussed that will require more volunteers or affect the work of existing volunteers.

- Executives build the case for volunteer engagement, both internally to staff and externally to potential volunteers and funders.

- Executives perform the actions outlined throughout this book on the pages titled "Executive Self-Assessment."

- The director of volunteer involvement and administrators design volunteer positions/internships to support executive activities, expect department heads to work with volunteers directly, and model effective partnering with volunteers.

- The director of volunteer involvement helps the executive apply best practices in volunteer management when working with the volunteers who sit on the board of directors or advisory council.

- The executive director directly recognizes volunteers as community representatives by periodically asking them to share their perspectives and requesting their help in spreading the word about the organization.

(continued)

Volunteer Involvement
and Senior Executives/Administrators

(continued)

- In presentations to the public and to funders, executives use stories about what impact volunteers make on the mission and clients of the organization.

- The director of volunteer involvement helps administrators keep up to date on volunteer trends and issues that may affect the organization's success at engaging volunteers, including board members.

- The director of volunteer involvement and top managers identify potential sources of volunteers and work together to maximize speaking engagements and community visits to disseminate materials about volunteer opportunities while also promoting the organization in other ways.

Volunteer Involvement and Programs/Services

Programs and client services are the core function of the organization—all other departments exist to enable these services to happen and the majority of volunteers will be recruited to help deliver these programs. Volunteer involvement staff must work closely with program managers and frontline staff to design and update volunteer opportunities, place the most qualified volunteers, and make certain that employees are trained to partner effectively with today's volunteers (and that volunteers are trained in how to team up with paid staff).

> *The following are ways volunteer involvement staff and program department heads should integrate their work so as to support each other, avoid duplication of effort, maximize each department's skills and expertise, and do what is best for successful volunteer involvement.*

- Work together on the design and updating of volunteer positions to serve in specific departments; create efficient systems for requesting new volunteer help.

- Provide training to all staff who (will) work with volunteers.

- Identify a liaison between the program and the volunteer resources staff; then provide training and ongoing communication to support this role.

- Determine clear expectations of staff working with volunteers and communicate those expectations to all staff.

- Evaluate the impact of volunteer engagement on staff, volunteers, and clients.

- Incorporate information on what volunteers accomplish into reports filed by the program or unit itself.

- Design ways to show appreciation to both program volunteers and the staff that supervise/support them.

- Provide ample opportunity for staff to share concerns regarding volunteer participation and to resolve issues together.

- Develop strategies to deal with difficult volunteer situations, especially those needing disciplinary action and prevent similar problems in the future.

- Create new opportunities for volunteers who have served for a length of time in one position and seek advancement.

Volunteer Involvement and Personnel, Human Resources, and Staff Education

Although usually separate departments, there are evident similarities between the work of an organization's volunteer involvement office and its human resources department: both are charged with recruiting and supporting the workforce serving the mission.

> *The following are ways these two functions should integrate their work so as to support each other, avoid duplication of effort, maximize each department's skills and expertise, and do what is best for successful volunteer involvement.*

- Meet regularly to evaluate staffing patterns, needs, and gaps to determine position openings for both volunteer and salaried staff.

- Develop policies and systems to best support staff who involve volunteers in their work.

- Design a training program and seek outside educational opportunities to develop staff skills in supervision, interviewing, delegation, etc. The training can focus on skill sets that enhance staff interaction with all personnel or focus on volunteer management and staff supervision skills separately.

- Coordinate general personnel policies and policies specific to volunteers—both should deal with staff and volunteer rights, expectations and responsibilities. Similarities and differences in policies for paid and unpaid workers should be considered and, if necessary, resolved.

- Design recruitment materials and techniques to gain the attention of prospective new staff, both paid and volunteer.

- Connect recruitment efforts on the organization's Web site so that employment opportunities and volunteer opportunities are both listed.

- Agree on consistent guidelines regarding volunteer staff being considered for paid staff opportunities.

- Design roles for volunteers to support the personnel function directly.

(continued)

Volunteer Involvement and Personnel, Human Resources, and Staff Education

(continued)

- Obtain resources (books, CDs, electronic training) which will train staff in their role of supervising volunteers and/or salaried staff.

- Agree on expectations of new hires about their previous experience partnering with volunteers, their openness to engage volunteers, and their level of training for working with volunteers that they have received.

- Plan for recognition events that highlight both volunteers and the contribution of paid staff who have been very effective in partnering with volunteers.

COLLABORATION STRATEGY

Volunteer Involvement and Development, Fundraising and Special Events

The cross-over between volunteers and donors is (or could be) significant, so both offices are potentially dealing with the same people. If invited properly, volunteers may become donors and donors may respond positively to invitations to volunteer. Both fundraising and volunteer involvement staff are out in the community making friends for the organization, so their messages about giving money and time should be integrated and consistent.

> *The following are ways these two functions should integrate their work so as to support each other, avoid duplication of effort, maximize each department's skills and expertise, and do what is best for successful volunteer involvement.*

- Connect routinely as allies, working together to highlight the organization's full range of services and its need for financial and human resources to support them.

- Acquire or tailor software (or other recordkeeping system) that will collect information on both volunteers and financial donors and create systems for updating, uncovering overlaps, avoiding duplication, and indicating when a donor expresses an interest in volunteering and vice versa.

- Regularly compare the time donor list to the money donor list to understand how they interconnect.

- Develop protocol for asking volunteers to become donors and work together to word special invitations to volunteers to contribute financially to the organization. Similarly, determine ways to encourage financial donors to consider volunteering or to spread the word about volunteer opportunities to their family members, friends, and colleagues.

- Develop materials that are useful to volunteers seeking to encourage in-kind support from their circle of friends and colleagues, applications to corporate Dollars for Doers opportunities, and other outreach.

- Create cross-postings on the organization's Web site, inviting those interested in volunteering to also contribute money and making sure that financial donors learn about opportunities to volunteer.

(continued)

Volunteer Involvement and Development, Fundraising and Special Events

(continued)

- Meet on a regular basis to discuss ways that volunteers can be useful in helping the organization raise funds and attract in-kind support.

- Meet to discuss and build the case to support volunteer initiatives through grant applications and other appeals to funders.

- Ensure that volunteers working on activities such as fundraisers, special events for the agency, etc., are well managed and integrated with direct service volunteers for such things as orientation and recognition.

- Build internal support for appropriate funding of volunteer engagement; work to establish an image that volunteering is a fundamental support of all organization programs and not in competition with those programs for funds.

- Work together to rebuild community support during times of public controversy about the organization.

Volunteer Involvement and Public Relations, Marketing, Community Outreach, Website and Social Media

All public and community relations outreach should incorporate some invitation to volunteer, just as all volunteer recruitment messages should convey a positive image of the organization consistent with public relations policies. Committed volunteers are an organization's best public relations agents and can be asked to serve as spokespeople to their circle of contacts, as well as representatives for the community's point of view providing feedback to the agency.

> *The following are ways these two functions should integrate their work so as to support each other, avoid duplication of effort, maximize each department's skills and expertise, and do what is best for successful volunteer involvement.*

- Prepare consistent messages to the media and the public; engage in joint efforts to connect with them to avoid confusion and build strong agency/media relations.

- Compare and coordinate community outreach schedules and events so as to share work and distribution of material and avoid duplication. Develop an ongoing calendar of key agency events and dates advertised to the public, including activities associated with volunteering.

- Mutually plan press releases and public service announcements regarding volunteer recruitment or recognition to assure the timing and quality of messages to the public.

- Brainstorm targeted marketing ideas to find appropriate volunteer candidates.

- Analyze the profile of current volunteers to identify their circles of friends, family, and business colleagues, particularly if those provide new contacts in diverse, hard-to-reach, or previously unconnected populations. In recognition that committed volunteers are the organization's best public relations advocates, develop ways to train volunteers to be effective spokespeople.

- Create volunteer-driven market surveys to assess the image of the organization in the community.

(continued)

Volunteer Involvement and Public Relations, Marketing, Community Outreach, Website and Social Media
(continued)

- Identify and communicate new community needs.

- Supply compelling public interest stories about volunteer impact for marketing staff to share with the public or other key constituents.

- Design a speaker and tour program (and recruit and train volunteers to staff it) for sharing clear and consistent messages to the public, raising the organization's profile and image.

- Work together to rebuild community support during times of public controversy about the organization.

- Ensure that the mention of volunteers is integrated into the organization's Web site, especially in terms of recognition of current volunteers and recruitment of new ones.

- Invite volunteers to contribute to Web content by keeping information updated, posting blog entries, and submitting stories and photographs.

- Identify volunteers who effectively utilize social media sites and work together to develop ways for the organization to make full use of such online opportunities.

Volunteer Involvement and Information Technology

Information technology (IT) evolves so rapidly that it is almost impossible for any IT staff to stay on top of the newest developments. Therefore, recruiting volunteers as advisers on specific software applications provides a continuous flow of updated information as needed. Skilled volunteers can help design Web pages, maintain content, and monitor Web postings from site visitors.

> *The following are ways these two functions should integrate their work so as to support each other, avoid duplication of effort, maximize each department's skills and expertise, and do what is best for successful volunteer involvement.*

- Ensure that the software used to manage volunteer involvement provides what is necessary for this purpose and is not simply an "add on" to software primarily designed for fundraising or client recordkeeping.

- Relate the databases of financial donors and volunteers so that, as needed, information can be compared and cross-referenced to maintain records on the total contributions of all supporters.

- Enable volunteers, as needed, to get password access to intranets or databases, designated e-mail addresses, and training in special software.

- With the public relations staff, design an attractive, informative Web presence for volunteers on the organization's Web site where current volunteer opportunities are posted and updated, and someone can express interest in volunteering via an online application or e-mail form.

- Develop systems for online support and training for volunteers.

Volunteer Involvement and Advocacy, Public Education, and Government Relations

Many volunteers are proponents of organizational causes and, if organized, can lead or greatly supplement advocacy to elected officials and others who have the power and influence to have an effect on the movement. Volunteers can be tremendous assets in carrying out public education and advocacy for the organization.

> *The following are ways these two functions should integrate their work so as to support each other, avoid duplication of effort, maximize each department's skills and expertise, and do what is best for successful volunteer involvement.*

- Attract and train volunteers to be advocates who target the community, elected officials, voters, etc., with the organization's mission-based messages. Develop ways for volunteers to take leadership in coordinating the citizen appeals of other volunteers.

- Train volunteers about critical issues and causes challenging the organization and its clients; provide updated information, useful data, and models for effective community outreach.

- Invite and equip all volunteers (regardless of assignment) to be messengers of education/advocacy for the organization, such as including them in blast e-mail action alerts.

- Offer opportunities for volunteer advocates who may also wish to deliver other volunteer services from within the organization, if they are made aware of the needs.

- Build social capital, facilitate civic participation, and provide a public voice as these are integral to both volunteer management and advocacy work.

- Keep updated on legal issues related to advocacy or lobbying when volunteers are representing a nonprofit or government organization.

- Make use of volunteers' status as private citizens and voters to ask them to write letters to legislators or even to lobby for a cause through personal office visits.

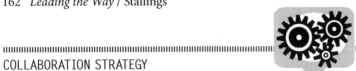

Volunteer Involvement and Finance/Accounting

Expert volunteers can assist with internal control, informal auditing, and investment decisions. The accounting staff can ensure that volunteer-run events handle cash and sales properly.

> *The following are ways these two functions should integrate their work so as to support each other, avoid duplication of effort, maximize each department's skills and expertise, and do what is best for successful volunteer involvement.*

- Plan for financial expenses and create accounting systems for volunteer-led events, including internal control, proper handling of cash, and more.

- Train volunteers on boards and committees in how to read financial reports, understand cash flow, etc.

- Create a uniform system of budgeting and accounting for the volunteer treasurer to use with the board.

- Determine a cost-benefit analysis and return-on-investment summary of volunteer contributions.

- Assist in developing a budget for effective volunteer engagement.

Volunteer Involvement and Legal Compliance and Risk Management

As part of the organization's workforce, volunteers must perform their work legally and safely and, in turn, be protected for their own safety and defense from liability. Working together, the legal and volunteer involvement staff can develop necessary legal forms, assess risk of all new volunteer positions, and provide risk management training.

> *The following are ways these two functions should integrate their work so as to support each other, avoid duplication of effort, maximize each department's skills and expertise, and do what is best for successful volunteer involvement.*

- Work together to create any forms that must meet legal requirements, such as:

  - Confidentiality statements

  - Parental permission forms

  - Liability waivers

  - Copyright agreements

- Ensure that all volunteer screening procedures fulfill legal requirements for background checks, obtaining references, etc.

- Conduct a risk analysis of any new volunteer assignment, re-assess current volunteer work, and develop instructions or training to enable volunteers to do their work safely.

- Weigh the benefits of allowing volunteers to do something potentially risky against the loss to the organization or clients of not allowing such activities to take place. Rather than reject a proposed volunteer role, work together to find the best legal and safe way to accomplish the needed service.

- Negotiate with the organization's insurance carrier to include coverage of volunteers or obtain excess insurance coverage for volunteers from another source. Make certain this coverage includes special event and one-time volunteers (not just volunteers in ongoing roles) as well as those driving an automobile as part of their assignment.

Volunteer Involvement and Maintenance, Security, and Physical Plant

Because of the way volunteer involvement activities occur, the maintenance staff provides support by keeping the organization's facility open odd hours, setting up furniture for group meetings, and generally keeping the offices attractive and safe for volunteers and staff. Volunteers can identify repair needs or potential hazards that need to be addressed for the health of clients and visitors.

> *The following are ways these two functions should integrate their work so as to support each other, avoid duplication of effort, maximize each department's skills and expertise, and do what is best for successful volunteer involvement.*

- Plan in advance for logistical needs for volunteer-run events, especially if held during hours the organization is not normally open.

- Develop security protocols to assure the safety of volunteers working in the building at off hours.

- Engage volunteers in group clean-ups and beautification projects.

- Establish standards and checklists for volunteer use of the facility.

- Prepare floor plans of optimal room set-ups for training, meetings, and other events.

A Guide to Expanding Volunteer Engagement

Each question below opens a window on possible new assignments for the *right* volunteers who can offer skills and talents different *from* those of the paid staff. Use this worksheet as a guide to design new volunteer positions within a department, unit, or function. Ask the director of volunteer involvement to share trends in volunteering, such as generational differences, to help staff consider the potential of new ways to engage volunteers.

1. **What are volunteers doing now** in our department/program/unit?

_____

_____

a. How were these roles developed?

_____

_____

b. When was the last time these tasks were assessed to see if they are still the most important ways volunteers can participate?

_____

_____

c. *Are* these roles, in fact, still critical?

_____

_____

OR *if there are no volunteers assigned to your work area......Why not?*

_____

_____

(continued)

A Guide to Expanding Volunteer Engagement
(continued)

a. Does anyone question the ability of qualified volunteers to contribute to the work? Based on what (facts, feelings, or other)?

_____

_____

b. How can we counter this resistance?

_____

_____

c. What might be a pilot test of something a volunteer can do in our area?

_____

_____

2. **Do paid staff have any tasks or responsibilities** that they might share with a volunteer, thus freeing them to do other things?

_____

_____

3. **What needs to be done** that current staff do not have the skills or time to do most effectively?

_____

_____

4. **What projects or activities are on our wish list** that stay on the back burner because there is no one to do them?

_____

_____

5. **What needs do our clients or consumers have** which we cannot fulfill with paid staff—and, if volunteers were found to help with these needs, the services staff provide would be improved or supported?

_____

_____

(continued)

A Guide to Expanding Volunteer Engagement
(continued)

6. **What service exists that would help the family, friends, or employers of our clients** and would support our primary work?

   _____

   _____

7. Might our staff or clients **benefit from any special area of expertise?** Fluency in a foreign language? Is there some advice we wish we could ask for when needed?

   _____

   _____

8. How could we benefit from volunteers who are **knowledgeable about online resources and social networking** to make best use of the Web for us?

   _____

   _____

9. Are we interested in finding qualified volunteers to **conduct any research?** Evaluations or assessments? Satisfaction surveys?

   _____

   _____

10. As a result of exploring the above questions, what new ways to engage volunteers have surfaced?

   _____

   _____

CHECKLIST

Starter Set of Ideas for Volunteer Talent to Support *You* – the Executive!

Use this list to get your creative juices flowing about possible volunteer positions that could assist with *your* workload. Check any that pique your interest and then discuss them with the director of volunteer involvement.

☐ Consultant in personnel benefits and policies

☐ Fundraising guru

☐ Researcher who can identify emerging trends in your field

☐ Transition specialist (new board, major staff turnover, etc.)

☐ Relocation expert

☐ Marketing manager

☐ Media contacts specialist

☐ Merger expert

☐ Educator in your field of service

☐ Advocacy coordinator

☐ Editor for the annual report

☐ Graphic designer

☐ Internet resource finder

☐ Office space organizer or interior decorator

☐ Ergonomic specialist to set up safe work sites

☐ Event planner

☐ Administrative assistant to help with your special projects

☐ Evaluator of the organization's programs

☐ Videographer to create orientation video for staff and volunteers

☐ Information technology specialist to evaluate your technology needs

☐ Executive coach

☐ Risk assessor

☐ Financial advisor with options for investments

☐ Experts of all types to educate the board

☐ Insurance and risk management specialist

☐ Trainers to bring some missing expertise to staff (such as social networking)

☐ Diversity specialist

☐ Grant proposal reviewer

☐ Speech writer/presentation developer

☐ Arbitration expert

☐ Communication specialist

☐ "Borrow An Expert" list of community specialists who agree to assist you in their area of expertise, when needed

☐ Board development coach

What other volunteer positions could you create to support your work as executive?

Do I integrate volunteers throughout the organization with these actions?

1. I reinforce our statement of philosophy/commitment about volunteer involvement by expecting every department, unit, and function to develop ways to partner with volunteers.

   ☐ Yes   ☐ No   ☐ Sometimes   ☐ Will now initiate   ☐ Not relevant

2. I monitor how fully integrated and inclusive the organization is regarding the role of volunteers within the organization.

   ☐ Yes   ☐ No   ☐ Sometimes   ☐ Will now initiate   ☐ Not relevant

3. I evaluate and reward middle managers on how they support their staff who work with volunteers and how they themselves work with volunteers.

   ☐ Yes   ☐ No   ☐ Sometimes   ☐ Will now initiate   ☐ Not relevant

4. I personally engage volunteers, other than the board of directors, to help with my own work.

   ☐ Yes   ☐ No   ☐ Sometimes   ☐ Will now initiate   ☐ Not relevant

5. I reinforce and reward staff/departments who effectively expand the engagement of volunteers.

   ☐ Yes   ☐ No   ☐ Sometimes   ☐ Will now initiate   ☐ Not relevant

6. I support the director of volunteer involvement in his/her efforts to advocate for volunteer engagement and to ensure best practices in volunteer management throughout the organization.

   ☐ Yes   ☐ No   ☐ Sometimes   ☐ Will now initiate   ☐ Not relevant

7. I encourage the training of all staff to design work and partner effectively with volunteers.

   ☐ Yes   ☐ No   ☐ Sometimes   ☐ Will now initiate   ☐ Not relevant

8. I encourage staff input into the planning and evaluation of volunteer engagement in the organization.

   ☐ Yes   ☐ No   ☐ Sometimes   ☐ Will now initiate   ☐ Not relevant

The Board's Role in Volunteer Engagement

I provide visibility for the volunteer pro-gram to the board so that they will understand its importance and support directing resources to it.

**Julie Packard, Executive Director
Monterey Bay Aquarium
Monterey, California**

Volunteering starts at the Board level. Each of our board members must have a passion for encouraging volunteers and volunteer potential. Our mission statement and procedures reflect that philosophy.

**Hillary Roberts, President
Blankie Depot
- Project Linus NJ, Inc.
Keyport, New Jersey**

CONTENTS

- **Introduction** to the Executive Role

- **Key Concept:** Why Volunteer Involvement Deserves Attention from the Board of Directors

- **Checklist:** 21 Ways a Board Can Demonstrate Support for Volunteer Involvement

- **Idea Stimulator:** Ways to Engage the Board of Directors in Volunteer Involvement

- **Idea Stimulator:** Questions the Board Might Ask to Keep Informed about Volunteers

- **Executive Self-Assessment:** *Do I facilitate the engagement of our board of directors in volunteer involvement with these actions?*

CONCEPTS IN DEPTH The tools in this section apply the concepts discussed at length in the book, *From the Top Down: The Executive Role in Successful Volunteer Involvement, 3rd edition,* by Susan J. Ellis (Philadelphia: Energize, Inc., 2010), specifically:

- Chapter 1: Why Volunteers?

- Chapter 2: Considerations in Planning – section on "The Role of the Board"

- Chapter 8: Executive-Level Volunteers – section on "The Board"

Introduction to the Executive Role

Ideally, an organization's governing body—the board of directors—oversees all activities of the organization including how volunteers contribute to the organization's goals and outcomes. Historically, the involvement of volunteers has rarely been on the agenda at board meetings. Infrequently do boards understand or discuss the philosophy behind or impact of engaging volunteers in the organization's mission. (Yet, board members are themselves the volunteer governing leaders of the organization!)

An agency executive who is truly committed to involving volunteers as partners in the mission must influence board members and facilitate their carrying out this responsibility. If there is a director of volunteer involvement in the organization, the executive can partner with her or him, benefiting from his or her expertise in volunteerism, to develop communication with the board about the work of volunteers. Once the board values the potential of effective volunteer engagement, it will be evident that they have a role in hiring an executive with a strong commitment to volunteer engagement, setting policy, allocating resources, and monitoring this part of the organization's work.

The tools in this section are meant to help the executive director prepare board members for their responsibilities in governing volunteer engagement just as they govern all other aspects of the organization:

- The first Idea Stimulator, "Why Volunteer Involvement Deserves Attention from the Board of Directors," makes the case for you, if you have any board members who initially resist spending time on the subject of volunteers.

- The Checklist, "21 Ways a Board Can Demonstrate Support for Volunteer Involvement," is offered for your use during a board meeting. Have the board consider how they currently engage themselves in supporting volunteers and what else they might do.

- The final two Idea Stimulators, "Ways to Engage the Board of Directors in Volunteer Involvement" and "Questions the Board Might Ask to Keep Informed about Volunteers," are further discussion starters—you need to determine the best methods of communication for your setting.

Also, the board is included in the collaboration strategies discussion presented in section seven.

> *"Historically, the involvement of volunteers has rarely been on the agenda at board meetings."*

Why Volunteer Involvement Deserves Attention from the Board of Directors

- Many volunteers are financial as well as time donors to the organization. Therefore, involving volunteers should be seen as part of any resource development strategy which the board surely monitors regularly.

- Volunteers are not free. Organizational resources are expended to engage them and so it's necessary to ensure that there is a legitimate return on investment. Conversely, it's important to allocate the tangible resources necessary to enable volunteers to contribute effectively. The board approves the organization's budget and so needs to understand this expense area.

- Volunteers are the "unpaid personnel department" and often outnumber employees. Since the board is aware of the staffing of the organization, this significant group of service contributors should not be invisible to them.

- Volunteers have enormous potential in public relations, fundraising, public education, legislative advocacy, and other community outreach functions. What volunteers are saying about the organization to their circles of family, friends, and contacts should be of interest to the board because it affects the organization's image.

- As community members with a demonstrated commitment to the organization, volunteers are a source of valuable information for planning and evaluation purposes, if someone asks their opinion or tries to understand their perspective.

- Board members are governance volunteers and should be involved in how they and other volunteers are engaged in the organization.

21 Ways a Board Can Demonstrate Support for Volunteer Involvement

Together as a board, discuss the items below and check those that you already accomplish. Consider how to accomplish the items that are left unchecked.

☐ Develop and disseminate our organization's statement of philosophy of volunteer engagement.

☐ Create and review policies related to volunteer involvement.

☐ Become knowledgeable about our current volunteer corps—who they are and what they do.

☐ Work with the director of volunteer involvement and the executive in determining the types of volunteers appropriate for our organization.

☐ Review, recommend, and endorse risk management practices and insurance coverage for volunteers.

☐ Review and support budget line items for volunteer involvement.

☐ Integrate volunteer involvement into all strategic planning.

☐ Regularly request reports on and then review volunteer engagement.

☐ Contribute to and/or review the evaluation of volunteer engagement.

☐ Allocate time at board meetings to discuss volunteer involvement.

☐ Actively recruit volunteers or make connections between potential volunteers and the organization, especially directing them to the leader of volunteer involvement.

☐ Spend a day shadowing a direct service volunteer working in our organization.

☐ Participate in volunteer recognition events where all volunteers (including ourselves as governance volunteers) are recognized as partners in the mission of the organization.

☐ In new board member orientation, include materials about volunteer engagement in our organization and how we, the board, support it.

(continued)

21 Ways a Board Can Demonstrate Support
for Volunteer Involvement
(continued)

☐ Hire an executive director who embraces the culture of volunteerism and then hold him or her accountable for supporting successful volunteer engagement.

☐ Ask questions such as: *How are we involving skilled community volunteers to contribute to this service/project?*

☐ Ask for the aggregate financial contribution of current and past volunteers (including significant in-kind gifts) to determine the link between volunteering and fundraising.

☐ Ask about the *impact* of volunteer involvement on the organization's mission —not merely for a tally of hours contributed multiplied by a wage equivalency cost.

☐ Invite one or more volunteers to a board meeting to share information about volunteering in the organization and to field questions from those with a volunteer perspective.

☐ Invite the director of volunteer involvement to a board meeting, at least annually. Then ask the director of volunteer involvement to facilitate a discussion about general trends in volunteerism and specific ways volunteering in the organization might be improved and expanded.

☐ Select an interested board member to be a liaison to volunteer engagement activities. She or he can serve on an advisory committee or volunteer management team, connect on a regular basis with the person leading volunteer engagement, and communicate in other appropriate ways both to and from the board.

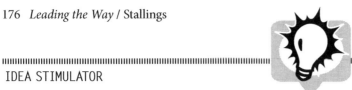

Ways to Engage the Board of Directors in Volunteer Involvement

The following are ways to ensure that essential information is exchanged between the board of directors and the volunteer involvement staff. Depending on the protocol of your organization, and the level of management at which the director of volunteer involvement is placed, contact may be direct or indirect, facilitated by the executive.

Method 1

The board selects one of its members to represent the board on an existing **volunteer involvement management team** or **volunteer advisory task force**. In this role, the board member brings pertinent items from the task force back to the board for information, input, response or action regarding volunteer engagement within the organization—and keeps the volunteer involvement office informed of board decisions or plans with potential to affect volunteers.

Method 2

The board forms its own **sub-committee on volunteer engagement** to consider the same agenda items as listed in Method 1 for a task force. The director of volunteer involvement staffs this committee and the sub-committee chair carries pertinent information between the board and the work of this sub-committee.

Method 3

The executive director receives regular reports on volunteer involvement from staff and carries it to the board for their response, input, or action. Here are ways this method might be implemented:

- The director of volunteer involvement reports directly to the executive so that communication is continuous, though once removed from the board.

- The director of volunteer involvement reports to someone who, in turn, reports to the executive—setting the communication with the board to "twice removed."

Note that, if the director of volunteer involvement is even lower on the organizational chart, the information that filters up to the board may be compromised by multiple participants in the communication chain.

(continued)

Ways to Engage the Board of Directors in Volunteer Involvement

(continued)

Method 4

The board requests specific information directly from specific individuals at specific times, such as the following:

- The board asks the executive or the director of volunteer involvement to present a report on volunteer involvement in person, available to answer any questions that arise.

- At the executive's prompting, the board invites the director of volunteer involvement to a board or committee meeting to present volunteer-specific issues or needs. The director of volunteer involvement is able to solicit help from board members to tap into their networks, places of employment, etc., to assist in recruitment.

- During strategic planning sessions, program planning or evaluations, the board, through the executive director, seeks input from the director of volunteer involvement and possibly from volunteers themselves.

- The director of volunteer involvement develops a format for reporting critical information about the organization's volunteer involvement to the board, on a regular basis. The information should be in writing and, at minimum once a year, the information should be presented in person.

- The board of directors requests volunteer engagement news/data to be communicated through agreed-upon existing channels, such as regular e-mails to the board, through a board listserv or other discussion group, as part of executive memos, etc.

- Volunteers are invited to designated board meetings where they report on their involvement and on the impact of that involvement on the mission of the organization.

Questions the Board Might Ask
to Keep Informed about Volunteers

After using the previous idea stimulator, "Ways to Engage the Board of Directors in Volunteer Involvement," share these questions to help the board identify what they could or should be monitoring about volunteer involvement. Both forms would be particularly useful prior to a scheduled presentation by the director of volunteer involvement.

- It is common to report the number of volunteers during a period and how much time they contributed. But this information is relatively meaningless without further probing. Questions that might illuminate the head-and-hour count are:

  - What is the demographic profile of the volunteer force?

    ▷ What diversity do they bring to our organization (age, gender, race, ethnicity, etc.)?

    ▷ What professions, occupations, and special training do they bring to us?

    ▷ From what geographic areas do they come?

  - From what sources have we obtained volunteers—individual applications, corporations, school-based programs, civic groups?

  - How many joined for the first time since the last report? How many left? Why did they leave? (Completed project? Left the area? Reason unknown?)

- What are some examples of new types of service initiated or provided with volunteers (e.g., consultants to train our advocacy volunteers)?

- What types of community partnerships have been formed during this period (e.g., liaison with nearby church youth group, nearest bank branch, etc.)?

- What are some examples of specific volunteer activities and their impact on the mission of our organization?

- What are ways that volunteer engagement has provided or generated positive publicity, effective public education, or expanded community outreach during the period?

(continued)

Questions the Board Might Ask
to Keep Informed about Volunteers

(continued)

- What is the aggregate of financial giving of our volunteers (current and former) during a specific time period?

- What issues, concerns, questions about volunteers need board attention/input/action/feedback?

- Is there any request for assistance in recruiting specific volunteers needed by the organization?

- What are some upcoming volunteer/staff training sessions that the board might attend?

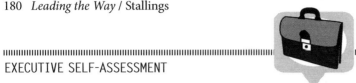

Do I facilitate the engagement of our board of directors in volunteer involvement with these actions?

1. I make it clear to the board that engaging volunteers is an essential strategy for capacity building toward meeting the mission of the organization.

    ☐ Yes   ☐ No   ☐ Sometimes   ☐ Will now initiate   ☐ Not relevant

2. I facilitate board involvement in carrying out these actions related to involving volunteers:

    a. Developing the organizational philosophy of volunteer engagement

        ☐ Yes   ☐ No   ☐ Sometimes   ☐ Will now initiate   ☐ Not relevant

    b. Creating policies related to volunteer involvement

        ☐ Yes   ☐ No   ☐ Sometimes   ☐ Will now initiate   ☐ Not relevant

    c. Determining types of volunteers appropriate for our organization

        ☐ Yes   ☐ No   ☐ Sometimes   ☐ Will now initiate   ☐ Not relevant

    d. Reviewing, recommending, and endorsing risk management/insurance for volunteer involvement

        ☐ Yes   ☐ No   ☐ Sometimes   ☐ Will now initiate   ☐ Not relevant

    e. Allocating funds for volunteer involvement in the budget

        ☐ Yes   ☐ No   ☐ Sometimes   ☐ Will now initiate   ☐ Not relevant

    f. Including volunteer involvement in agency-wide strategic planning

        ☐ Yes   ☐ No   ☐ Sometimes   ☐ Will now initiate   ☐ Not relevant

    g. Evaluating volunteer engagement and assessing its return on investment

        ☐ Yes   ☐ No   ☐ Sometimes   ☐ Will now initiate   ☐ Not relevant

    h. Allocating time at board meetings to discuss volunteer involvement

        ☐ Yes   ☐ No   ☐ Sometimes   ☐ Will now initiate   ☐ Not relevant

    i. Participating in volunteer orientation sessions

        ☐ Yes   ☐ No   ☐ Sometimes   ☐ Will now initiate   ☐ Not relevant

(continued)

Do I facilitate the engagement of our board of directors in volunteer involvement with these actions?

(continued)

j. Actively recruiting volunteers or connecting potential volunteers to the organization

☐ Yes   ☐ No   ☐ Sometimes   ☐ Will now initiate   ☐ Not relevant

k. Spending a day in the shoes of a direct service volunteer working in the organization

☐ Yes   ☐ No   ☐ Sometimes   ☐ Will now initiate   ☐ Not relevant

l. Participating in volunteer recognition events where all volunteers (including governance volunteers) are recognized as partners in the mission

☐ Yes   ☐ No   ☐ Sometimes   ☐ Will now initiate   ☐ Not relevant

m. Including information about volunteer participation in new board member orientation

☐ Yes   ☐ No   ☐ Sometimes   ☐ Will now initiate   ☐ Not relevant

n. Participating in a visioning session for our organization's volunteer program of the future

☐ Yes   ☐ No   ☐ Sometimes   ☐ Will now initiate   ☐ Not relevant

3. I facilitate or require regular communication between volunteer involvement staff and the board.

☐ Yes   ☐ No   ☐ Sometimes   ☐ Will now initiate   ☐ Not relevant

4. I request a board representative to sit on a volunteer management team/task force and/or volunteer advisory committee as the liaison from the board to the volunteer engagement effort.

☐ Yes   ☐ No   ☐ Sometimes   ☐ Will now initiate   ☐ Not relevant

5. I show appreciation/recognition to the board as governing *volunteers* serving the organization.

☐ Yes   ☐ No   ☐ Sometimes   ☐ Will now initiate   ☐ Not relevant

Ensuring Legal Compliance and Managing Risk When Involving Volunteers

*A*s an executive, it's my job to not only be the main cheerleader for our volunteer program, but also the toughest critic. I have to constantly think about what can go wrong and how can we control and minimize risks to our organization and our clients, staff and volunteers. It may not be fun, but thinking about risk management is critical to making sure we achieve our mission both today and in the future.

John L. Lipp,
President and CEO
Pets Are Wonderful Support
(PAWS)
San Francisco, California

As an executive director and the head of a volunteer center, I need to be informed about and in compliance with national, state and local laws governing volunteering. I don't want anything to compromise our organization's volunteer engagement—or that of any organization, program or initiative to which we refer prospective volunteers.

Sue Carter, Executive Director
Volunteer San Diego
San Diego, CA

CONTENTS

- **Introduction** to the Executive Role

- **Checklist:** Are Volunteers Included in Our Legal and Risk Planning?

- **Action Steps:** Limiting Risk in Volunteer Involvement

- **Example:** Sample General Policy Statement on Risk Management

- **Key Concept:** Create a Risk-Aware Corporate Culture

- **Idea Stimulator:** Some Questions to Ask Your Attorney or Legal Department

- **Idea Stimulator:** Stereotypes, Misinformation, and Poor Advice Sometimes Expressed by Legal Advisors...and Suggestions for Executive Response to Them

- **Executive Self-Assessment:** *Do I ensure legal compliance and proper risk management of volunteer involvement with these actions?*

CONCEPTS IN DEPTH

The tools in this section apply the concepts discussed at length in the book, *From the Top Down: The Executive Role in Successful Volunteer Involvement, 3rd edition,* by Susan J. Ellis (Philadelphia: Energize, Inc., 2010), specifically:

- Chapter 9: Risk, Liability, and Other Legal Issues

Introduction to the Executive Role

egal liability and risk management have become critical—and fearful—topics in today's management environment. Some organizations choose to keep their fingers crossed and their heads in the sand, hoping that they will avoid any unpleasant surprises. But avoidance does not get rid of real philosophical and legal issues.

• Are we doing the most we can to comply with the law and keep everyone safe?

• Do we tend to scale back important services that expose us to a high level of risk? Can we do anything to diminish such risk without detriment to our services?

• How can we know that we are operating in a safe fashion? How safe is safe?

Such important questions must be dealt with on an organization-by-organization basis, in consultation with expert legal and insurance advisors.

First, executives must include volunteers on the agenda in any legal or risk management discussion. It may be necessary to educate attorneys, risk managers, and insurance agents about how your organization involves volunteers and what type of roles volunteers play. Explain your careful, ongoing risk management practices and counter any stereotypes or prejudices these advisers might show about volunteer participation. Most importantly, be alert for knee-jerk risk avoidance statements such as, "You shouldn't use volunteers in that capacity. It's too risky." A responsibly run volunteer program can have excellent safety practices.

As executive, you must personally understand potential risk involving volunteers and then provide support and oversight to ensure full compliance among staff and volunteers with the organization's risk management rules. Because there are no risk-free guarantees in any activity in life, it is also prudent to explore or purchase any needed protections offered by available insurance policies.

This chapter only presents basic information about risk identification and prevention. It is not intended to give legal advice. Rather, it offers some tools to spur thinking and action in this arena.

A great resource for risk management and legal issues in the United States is the Nonprofit Risk Management Center, http://www.nonprofitrisk. org. They provide many materials focused on volunteer involvement risks as one of their featured topics. (A wonderful role for a volunteer to assist the executive would be to visit this site regularly and report on any new information or publications that deal with volunteers and risk management.)

> *"A responsibly run volunteer program can have excellent safety practices."*

CHECKLIST

Are Volunteers Included in Our Legal and Risk Planning?

> Volunteers are easily omitted or neglected when formulating organizational policies, including legal compliance and risk management decisions. Go through the statements below and check off the areas in which you feel volunteers have been thoughtfully considered. Items left unchecked may become a "to-do list" for executive action.

Legal Compliance

☐ We are informed about and in compliance with national, state/provincial, and local laws governing volunteer involvement.

☐ We apply the same non-discrimination policies to volunteers as to staff.

☐ We clearly differentiate between work for which someone is paid and work for which someone volunteers.

☐ Our volunteer application form asks only questions that would also be permitted on a prospective employee application.

☐ We have clarified how employee policies and procedures do or do not apply to volunteers.

☐ We comply with all laws requiring special screening such as criminal background and child abuse checks for volunteers in roles with vulnerable populations.

☐ We obtain parental permission when volunteers are underage.

☐ We provide access to any volunteer with a disability.

☐ We reimburse volunteers for actual expenses and do not provide lump-sum payments that might be taxed as income to the volunteer.

☐ We obtain permission from volunteers to use their photographs or full names in publicity.

☐ When a volunteer develops intellectual property for us, we clarify copyright and usage arrangements.

(continued)

Are Volunteers Included in Our Legal and Risk Planning?
(continued)

Risk Management

☐ We keep accurate records of who is a volunteer and what she or he does at our request. This includes knowing what volunteers do off-site or online on our behalf.

☐ We carry out safety facility inspections annually to uncover potential risks in the work areas of staff and volunteers.

☐ Volunteers are made aware of the boundaries of their position descriptions. (What they can and cannot do. Where they should and should not be.)

☐ We provide training for volunteers in the proper use of any equipment that might be hazardous.

☐ Volunteers are included in and have been informed about emergency evacuation procedures (fire or other crisis).

☐ Volunteers are included in our notification plan for closure due to bad weather and other emergency messages.

☐ We train volunteers on the importance of confidentiality.

☐ We do not permit anyone to volunteer "casually," without going through the volunteer involvement office.

☐ We give volunteers important policies in writing and keep those updated.

☐ We create clear instruction sheets to guide volunteers who work with us for a single day at a time or who may be filling in for someone else.

☐ We have sufficient controls for handling finances in events involving staff and volunteers.

☐ Volunteers sign a statement that they have read, understand, and agree to follow the procedures and policies in the volunteer/personnel manual.

☐ We have clear policies on how/who can talk to the media and how our logo can be used.

☐ We have policies and systems to prevent fraud by any staff or volunteer who has access to finances of the organization.

(continued)

Are Volunteers Included in Our Legal and Risk Planning?
(continued)

Labor Relations

☐ We have a grievance procedure for volunteers.

☐ We include a statement about the role of volunteers in any labor union agreement we reach.

☐ We have a written conflict of interest statement that includes both paid and unpaid staff.

☐ We do not violate the U.S. Fair Labor Standards Act by expecting employees to volunteer above and beyond their paid work duties.

☐ We have created guidelines for volunteer involvement if there is a labor strike.

☐ We have clear policies and procedures for volunteer dismissal.

Insurance

☐ We provide insurance or other coverage for volunteers who get hurt while working with us.

☐ We are covered by insurance for any act by a volunteer that causes injury or damage to others.

☐ We carry appropriate auto insurance for any volunteer drivers.

☐ We carry Errors and Omissions Insurance for our board members (and have an indemnification clause covering them in our by-laws).

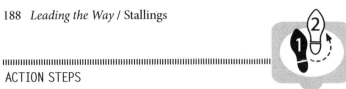

Limiting Risk in Volunteer Involvement

The following are steps organizations can take to diminish the chance of risk when volunteers are involved in carrying out their assigned activities.

Step 1

Develop volunteer position descriptions that support your risk management strategy.

Each volunteer position description should:

- Establish and communicate what a person is expected to do and not do.

- Focus on qualifications for the job, indicating specific abilities and skill levels.

- List activities involved in the position so that these can be assessed for potential risk and possible orientation and training content to assure the safety of volunteers and others around them.

- Serve as a tool for choosing the proper level of screening and discourage unqualified individuals from becoming volunteers.

- Provide documentation, when necessary, to show that a volunteer acted outside of his or her assigned duties.

Step 2

Screen and interview prospective volunteers with reducing risk in mind.

- Interview volunteers to learn what skills they do or do not have and match them to assignments accordingly.

- Use a fair, structured procedure of screening to avoid haphazard and arbitrary placements.

- For positions where volunteers will be working with vulnerable populations, use multiple screening interviews conducted by different people to increase the chance of revealing red flag responses.

- Ask critical questions more than once, in different ways.

- Verify information, if warranted, including checking references.

(continued)

Limiting Risk in Volunteer Involvement
(continued)

- Gather all data before making final judgments.

- Make certain that information you gather is necessary and appropriate for the position.

- Provide full disclosure about all screening procedures which may be used to consider candidates.

- Be consistent. Screen all candidates for the same volunteer position alike, using the same set of interview questions and screening techniques.

- Conduct criminal background checks on volunteers who interact with children, the elderly or others who might be vulnerable to abuse.

- Interview volunteers about any medical conditions that might prohibit them from safely completing or from doing certain tasks required of the position (e.g., allergies or back problems).

Step 3

Provide quality training and orientation to new volunteers.

- Include all safety rules and emergency procedures in orientation and training sessions.

- Explain the process of recording donated volunteer time and why it is important for the organization to have such records for insurance and other purposes.

- Share information about insurance coverage provided to volunteers, if applicable.

- Provide written information regarding the organization's mission and values, personnel, risk management and other pertinent volunteer policies.

- Introduce the volunteer to his or her direct supervisor/leader and explain where to direct any complaints or problems.

- Train volunteers to ensure that they can perform their tasks skillfully and safely.

- Supervise and otherwise support all volunteers so that they are empowered to do an effective job.

(continued)

Limiting Risk in Volunteer Involvement
(continued)

- Hold staff supervisors accountable for making sure volunteers perform their duties in the way they have been trained.

- Give volunteers timely and specific feedback so that their behavior is reinforced or changed.

- Transfer or dismiss volunteers, if warranted.

- Do not assign new work to volunteers who have not been adequately screened or prepared.

- Provide in-service training to keep volunteer skills up to date.

Step 4

Inspect your facility for potential hazards or risk.

- When volunteers are assigned to a new work location or when you select a site for a special event, conduct a potential hazard inspection for such issues as slip and fall accidents, poor fire protection, poor security, poor lighting, and more.

- Make whatever safety improvements necessary.

- Develop an incident reporting system.

Step 5

Create and enforce policies and procedures relating to risk management.

- Write a general policy statement explaining your organization's approach to risk management. (See next page for example.)

- Establish a standard for behavior and a common body of knowledge such as steps in reporting an accident.

- Support unpleasant, but necessary requirements such as wearing a hair net when working with food.

- When orienting and training staff, volunteers, board members and clients, give them written policies and procedures.

- Ensure that volunteers have been considered in all organization policies and mentioned specifically whenever a policy applies to them.

(continued)

Limiting Risk in Volunteer Involvement
(continued)

- Identify which policies apply equally to employees and volunteers, and write additional policies that may apply only to volunteers or to employees when they work with volunteers.

- As appropriate, reduce the opportunity for risky behavior by establishing limits and boundaries for volunteers (such as not permitting volunteers to take clients to their own homes).

- Consider policies for areas such as:

  ▷ Who can volunteer

  ▷ Training, certification, in-service requirements for designated positions

  ▷ Sexual harassment and anti-discrimination rules

  ▷ Complaint procedures and due process

  ▷ Media relations (Who speaks for the organization?)

  ▷ Use of organization's name and logo

  ▷ Emergency procedures

  ▷ Suspension and dismissal policies

  ▷ Financial controls

  ▷ Confidentiality issues

  ▷ Volunteer screening procedures

  ▷ Working conditions

  ▷ Liability and accident insurance for volunteers and its relation to their personal insurance

- Define actions to be taken in the event a volunteer is injured, injures someone or damages someone's property.

Step 6

Consider purchasing insurance that covers volunteer activity

- Ask your current insurance carrier to clarify, in writing, if volunteers are covered in all ways that employees, clients, or visitors are covered, and in what circumstances volunteers are not. Possible special insurance needs include:

(continued)

Limiting Risk in Volunteer Involvement
(continued)

> ▷ Expenses due to accidents, injuries, and personal liability of volunteers

> ▷ Liability for acts of volunteers that result in someone else being harmed or property damage

> ▷ Excess automobile insurance for volunteers who drive on your behalf

> ▷ Indemnification for board volunteers and officers

> ▷ Special event coverage

- If necessary, investigate and purchase additional insurance, particularly to provide coverage for volunteers in excess of personal insurance they may carry.

- Explore whether or not volunteers who will handle cash need to be bonded.

Sample General Policy Statement on Risk Management

Effective risk management begins with the understanding, by everyone in the organization, that the effort is important, that the effort is supported by senior staff and the board, and that everyone is expected to uphold that effort. The sample policy is offered by The CIMA Companies, Inc. (www.cimaworld.com), which administers the Volunteers Insurance Service (VIS®) program:

(Name of organization) is subject to certain risks that affect our ability to operate, serve customers and protect assets. These include risks to employees and volunteers, liability to others, and risks to property.

Controlling these risks through a formal program is necessary for the well-being of the organization and everyone in it. The jobs and services the organization provides, the safety of the workplace and other benefits all depend to an extent on our ability to control risks.

Management has the ultimate responsibility to control risks. Control includes making decisions regarding which risks are acceptable and how to address those that are not. Those decisions can be made only with the participation of the entire workforce, because each of us understands the risks of his or her own tasks better than anyone else in the organization does. Each is responsible for reporting any unsafe conditions he or she sees. Also, each is encouraged to suggest ways in which we can operate more safely. We are committed to the careful consideration of everyone's suggestions, and to taking appropriate action to address risks.

Accidents and other situations involving loss or near-loss will be investigated as part of the effort to manage risks.

Every employee's and volunteer's performance will be evaluated, in part, according to how he or she complies with this policy.

Written by William R. Henry, Jr., director of communication for The CIMA Companies, Inc. Originally published in the Everyone Ready® *Self-Instruction Guide, "Insurance and Risk Management Issues For Volunteer Programs – What Every Decision Maker Should Know," © 2007, Energize, Inc.*

Create a Risk-Aware Corporate Culture

Written by Linda L. Graff, in her book *Better Safe... Risk Management in Volunteer Programs & Community Service* (Dundas, ON: Linda Graff & Associates, Inc., 2003). Reprinted with permission. Learn more at http://www.lindagraff.ca.

Welcome Communication

- Create opportunities to talk about risk.
- Help volunteers understand that risk is a normal part of doing business.
- Help them to become conscious of risks in their day-to-day environment.
- Encourage identification and reporting of risks wherever volunteers work.
- Make sure that paid staff feel comfortable reporting risks related to volunteer involvement.
- Communicate that risk management creates a safer work environment for all.

Educate

- Enhance risk identification skills through ongoing training, case conferences, in-service sessions, supervisory meetings, performance reviews, etc.
- Help volunteers to understand the full range of risk control options available in their own area of the workplace, including the small things that everybody can do to increase safety.
- Help them to know what issues should be reported, and to whom.

Appreciate

- Reward everyone who identifies and reports risks.
- Make risk management a competency area and build it into the volunteer performance management system.
- Announce successes, publicly acknowledge and reward volunteers' efforts to make the workplace and the organization's services safer for everyone.
- Attention to risk management and good risk reduction ideas could become the basis of a special annual volunteer recognition award.

Implement

- People need to see that their efforts bring results.
- Follow up on all suggestions.
- Implement risk control strategies and report back to the risk identifier on actions that have been taken.

Some Questions to Ask
Your Attorney or Legal Department

It is better to be prepared and knowledgeable about what is legal, risky, or not—even if we are afraid of the answer we might get from legal advisors. Just remember that *asking* a question does not assume there is a problem—and be sure that your lawyer *does research* into what the real answers are about volunteers in your field of work and in your legal jurisdiction. Also, seek out an insurance agent who carries policies specifically designed for volunteers. The following is a starter set of generic queries:

1. Which employment laws apply to volunteers and the work they do? Under what circumstances might a volunteer be legally considered an "employee"?

2. Even if not directly applicable, should we follow general labor laws (such as the Fair Labor Standards Act in the United States) when designing work for volunteers? Are there any other regulations affecting the parameters of the work that can be done by volunteers?

3. Are there any screening or background check requirements to which we must adhere in bringing new volunteers on board? Are we legally able to turn down offers by volunteers to serve our organization?

4. What documents should we be asking volunteers or their guardians to sign? (Liability waivers? Confidentiality agreements? Permission slips?)

5. How can we practice effective risk management in developing assignments for volunteers and in training volunteers to fill them?

6. Who is liable for damage or injury caused by a volunteer?

7. Who is liable for injury to a volunteer?

8. Do we need actual insurance coverage ("errors and omissions") for the board of directors or are we safe with simply a board member indemnification clause in our by-laws?

9. If volunteers are involved in the production of intellectual property, who owns the product and the rights to use the material in the future?

10. Can we fire volunteers?

11. What expenses can we reimburse to a volunteer (and how) without it becoming taxable income?

12. When we collaborate with community groups, corporations, or schools, whose insurance coverage applies?

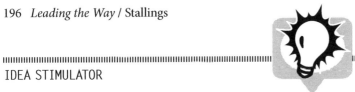

Stereotypes, Misinformation, and Poor Advice
Sometimes Expressed by Legal Advisors

Stereotype, Misinformation, Poor Advice	Possible Response by Executive
We should dispense with all volunteer activity. It brings too much risk exposure to the organization.	You are advising risk avoidance, not risk management. The benefits of involving qualified volunteers in a safe way far outweigh worst-case scenario thinking. We risk more by not engaging the community in our work.
Volunteers should not hold positions which give them access to confidential information.	Confidential information should not be shared with anyone who does not have a need to know, whether paid or unpaid. Volunteers can be trained to uphold confidentiality related to work to which they are assigned.
Volunteers are more accident prone than employees. You should purchase lots of insurance to protect yourself against lawsuits involving volunteers.	There is no evidence that volunteers are inherently riskier than employees are. Usually what is needed is excess insurance coverage, which is available at low cost.
Board members should not sit on a board unless it offers Errors and Omissions Insurance.	This is a personal decision for each board member, who may consider the likely risks and potential liabilities.
There are labor unions active in this organization and therefore I would not recommend engaging volunteers in your work.	Countless organizations have both union employees and volunteers. The key is discussing volunteer work design with labor leaders during contract negotiations and not using volunteers as strike breakers.
All volunteers need extensive background checks and should be finger printed.	Such a requirement depends on the setting and population served, but even when working with vulnerable populations, such screening is mainly needed for volunteers who will have direct, individual contact with clients. Episodic or indirect service volunteers should not be permitted non-monitored interaction with clients, but do not need all the checks, either.

(continued)

Stereotypes, Misinformation, and Poor Advice Sometimes Expressed by Legal Advisors

(continued)

Stereotype, Misinformation, Poor Advice	Possible Response by Executive
You should never allow volunteers to work directly with vulnerable clients. It is far too risky.	To whom? To the client, should the volunteer do something wrong? To the volunteer, should the client make an accusation? To the organization should a relative complain? If the organization serves vulnerable clients, then it is legitimate to recruit the right, qualified (skills and temperament) volunteers to do so, too—and train and supervise them appropriately.
It is illegal for volunteers to do any of the same work that is carried out by paid staff.	This is a misinterpretation of the Fair Labor Standards Act in that qualified and willing volunteers can do many of the same tasks and activities as employees, but should not be recruited as substitutes for previously-paid positions. Almost every type of work done by an employee is done somewhere else by a volunteer, and vice versa, depending on the situation.
There are many liability law suits involving inappropriate behavior on the part of volunteers and thus I would recommend staying away from engaging volunteers.	Actually, the number of lawsuits involving volunteers is quite low and there is no evidence that a well-managed volunteer involvement strategy would place our organization into risk of legal action.

Do I ensure legal compliance and proper risk management of volunteer involvement with these actions?

1. I support an annual risk management assessment of our organization and include issues of volunteer involvement.

    ☐ Yes   ☐ No   ☐ Sometimes   ☐ Will now initiate   ☐ Not relevant

2. I put risk control strategies in place for any risk surfaced in this annual assessment.

    ☐ Yes   ☐ No   ☐ Sometimes   ☐ Will now initiate   ☐ Not relevant

3. I review strategies to manage most of the risks associated with engaging volunteers.

    ☐ Yes   ☐ No   ☐ Sometimes   ☐ Will now initiate   ☐ Not relevant

4. I, along with the board of directors, develop policies and procedures that identify and mitigate risks associated with volunteer involvement, guide volunteers in their work, and guide employees in partnering with volunteers.

    ☐ Yes   ☐ No   ☐ Sometimes   ☐ Will now initiate   ☐ Not relevant

5. I am confident that our volunteer management practices meet current standards, particularly in risk areas such as screening, orientation, training, supervision, discipline and dismissal.

    ☐ Yes   ☐ No   ☐ Sometimes   ☐ Will now initiate   ☐ Not relevant

6. I, along with the board, stay current on all changes in legislation and legal precedents that may affect any aspect of the work that volunteers do for us.

    ☐ Yes   ☐ No   ☐ Sometimes   ☐ Will now initiate   ☐ Not relevant

7. I make sure that immediate and appropriate action is taken whenever a risk related to volunteer involvement is identified or an incident occurs.

    ☐ Yes   ☐ No   ☐ Sometimes   ☐ Will now initiate   ☐ Not relevant

(continued)

Do I ensure legal compliance and proper risk management of volunteer involvement with these actions?

(continued)

8. I challenge attorneys, risk managers, and insurance agents whenever they base their assessment of potential risks of volunteer activities on negative and incorrect opinions of how we manage volunteers in our organization.

    ☐ Yes   ☐ No   ☐ Sometimes   ☐ Will now initiate   ☐ Not relevant

9. I believe that volunteer contributions are essential and do all that I can to manage risks so as not to eliminate any volunteer positions that serve our mission.

    ☐ Yes   ☐ No   ☐ Sometimes   ☐ Will now initiate   ☐ Not relevant

Monitoring, Evaluating, and Improving Volunteer Involvement

CONTENTS

CONCEPTS IN DEPTH

The tools in this section apply the concepts discussed at length in the book, *From the Top Down: The Executive Role in Successful Volunteer Involvement, 3rd edition,* by Susan J. Ellis (Philadelphia: Energize, Inc., 2010), specifically:

- Chapter 10: Evaluating the Impact of Volunteers
- Chapter 11: The Financial Value of Volunteer Contributions

||||||||||||||||||||||||||||||||||||||||||||||||||||||||||||||||||||||||||||||||||||||||||||||||||||||||||||||||||||||||||||||||||||||||||||||

Introduction to the Executive Role

Every executive needs and wants to know how her or his organization is doing, from a range of perspectives. Undoubtedly, you conduct a variety of formal and informal evaluations each year. Are you also assessing volunteer involvement?

I urge you to make sure volunteers are not overlooked or invisible in any evaluation process. Further, on a regular basis, you need to focus on examining the impact that volunteers are having on your organization's mission and operations. How many volunteers you have is unconnected to the value of what they do. Do you really know what that is?

The whole purpose of assessment is to inform the next round of planning, the subject of sections one and two—so we've come full circle. This is particularly pertinent because in order to evaluate something you have to know, at the start, what you are setting out to do. The steps of evaluation that require executive action are:

1. Articulate why you want to engage volunteers and goals and objectives for the work you will ask them to do. What will success look like?

2. Ensure that a data gathering and recordkeeping system is in place that collects information that will be the documentation for the end-of-period assessment.

3. Receive, monitor, and respond to regular reports about volunteers during the period.

4. Give input on and approve the assessment goals, methods, and questions used to evaluate the impact of volunteer contributions.

5. Once the evaluation findings are reported, allocate additional resources or make suggested changes so that the organization has the most effective volunteer involvement possible.

6. Whenever you evaluate the organization as a whole, or one program or project, be sure to include assessment questions about volunteer contributions as well.

Again, if you do not plan to act on what is learned, why invest the time and resources needed to carry out an effective evaluation?

Lack of funds is frequently cited as a reason that an organization cannot afford to carry out a meaningful evaluation of volunteer involvement. However, this is more a matter of will than money. In fact, the right volunteer (possibly a college intern studying evaluation methods) could spearhead the assessment effort, reporting directly to you or the director of volunteer involvement. This models effective engagement of a highly skilled volunteer while gaining important information about volunteer impact.

This section asks you to consider why evaluation is necessary to build strong volunteer engagement, suggests questions to ask in monitoring performance, considers cost-benefit analysis, and presents four key methods for evaluating volunteer involvement.

> *"...focus on examining the impact that volunteers are having on your organization's mission and operations."*

15 Reasons to Evaluate Volunteer Involvement

1. To identify and celebrate volunteer success stories and share them with significant stakeholders—volunteers themselves (including the board), paid staff, donors and funders, the media, and the community at large.

2. To identify what is going well in order to continue doing more of it.

3. To discover barriers and challenges that hinder effective volunteer involvement.

4. To obtain fresh ideas and suggestions to do even better in the future.

5. To prove to volunteers that they, indeed, make a difference.

6. To get buy-in from paid staff by showing how the time they spend supporting volunteers matters.

7. To show appreciation (recognition) to volunteers and paid staff by giving them the opportunity to participate in the evaluation and then feel pride in the results.

8. To determine appropriate allocation of funds to build the capacity of the organization to support volunteer engagement.

9. To utilize the information about the impact of volunteer involvement to recruit new volunteers.

10. To educate staff and volunteers about what elements are involved in determining the success of volunteer involvement.

11. To assess return-on-investment of the costs versus the value of volunteer contributions.

12. To anticipate concerns that can be addressed to avert significant future problems.

13. To diffuse the negative feelings of a few staff or volunteers if the evaluation does not find similar negative reactions shared by many others in the organization.

14. To be the basis for a staff retreat to work through barriers keeping volunteer engagement from reaching its potential in your organization.

15. To address whatever issues the evaluation surfaces.

Possible Questions for Assessing Volunteer Involvement

The best way to monitor and assess the current involvement of volunteers so that you can evaluate its quality and effectiveness is to **ask the right questions** on an ongoing basis. Below is a starter set of questions to discuss with the person leading volunteer engagement in your organization.

Put a checkmark next to the questions you currently ask (and receive answers to). Then review the items you did not check and consider whether you ought to start getting those answers, too.

☐ Did we set goals for what volunteers are going to accomplish before we started?

☐ Has volunteer involvement reached the goals we established for this period (and if not, why not)?

☐ How effectively or successfully were the goals met?

☐ How many volunteers were engaged in activities supporting our mission and in what range of activities?

☐ Are volunteers integrated into all functions of the organization and do they work with staff at all levels (frontline and management)?

☐ What are the demographics of the volunteer work force in our organization? Are they the same as the demographics of our community or the clients we serve?

☐ How many volunteers serve in volunteer positions that are long term, short term, episodic, and spontaneous?

☐ Do we retain volunteers for the period of time to which they commit when they start to work with us? If not, why not?

☐ Do we engage highly skilled and pro bono volunteers?

☐ What would be the wage-equivalency cost of the time volunteers contribute to us and what is the *true* value of the benefits we derive from their participation?

☐ What are the costs of supporting volunteers?

(continued)

Possible Questions for Assessing Volunteer Involvement

(continued)

☐ Were the benefits of volunteer involvement worth these costs? How?

☐ Which staff/departments engage volunteers and how well?

☐ Which staff/departments do not involve volunteers and why?

☐ What is the general satisfaction level of volunteers serving our organization?

☐ What is the level of paid staff satisfaction with volunteer participation?

☐ What has been the feedback from clients on the engagement of volunteers in service to them?

☐ What are the major strengths and successes of our volunteer engagement?

☐ What is the impact/outcome of engaging volunteers (e.g., what has changed or improved with our clients as a result of involving volunteers in our mission)?

☐ What are the key challenges and weaknesses of our volunteer engagement?

☐ What were the successes and challenges of engaging volunteers in special short-term projects or single days of service/special events?

☐ What is the impact of volunteers on raising money? What is the correlation of our money donors to our time donors?

☐ What volunteer assignments should we stop doing and why?

☐ What new needs might volunteers tackle?

☐ Are we asking questions about volunteer involvement in all other evaluations we conduct on any aspect of the work of the organization, including assessment of special projects to which volunteers have contributed time and skills?

Ways to Value Volunteer Contributions

> Executives frequently want to assess the financial benefits of engaging volunteers, which can be interesting, if not always insightful. Keep in mind that monetary worth is not the only "value" volunteers bring to your organization. Here are some things to consider when assessing worth.

Cost-Benefit Analysis

You can compare what you spent on volunteer involvement and the wage-equivalency value of the work volunteers contributed. Designate a time period to study and determine what your organization spent in that period to involve volunteers. Include:

- Salaries and benefits of both the volunteer involvement staff and the percentage of time spent by other staff in managing volunteers

- Direct program costs (recruitment, recognition, training, etc.)

- Volunteer support costs (insurance, reimbursed expenses)

- Indirect program costs and overhead (space, equipment, etc.)

Then calculate the financial contributions made by volunteers in the period. Include:

- An estimated financial value of the number of volunteers hours contributed, which you can determine by a number of methods, including:

  - Researching the marketplace wage replacement cost for each volunteer position

  - Using the median wage figure provided by the Department of Labor

  - Calculate an average hourly wage for your entire payroll and use that figure for volunteer time, too

  - Using an amount calculated by an outside body, such as is done annually in the United States by the Independent Sector (found at http://www.independentsector.org/programs/research/volunteer_time.html, reported in 2009 as $20.25/hour)

  - Whenever possible, avoid using the minimum wage, as this is almost always an under-valuation of the work most volunteers do

- Money raised through the efforts of volunteers (such as special events and donor solicitations)

- Actual cash contributions by volunteers

(continued)

Ways to Value Volunteer Contributions
(continued)

- In-kind, unreimbursed donations (equipment, mileage, furniture) given or accessed by volunteers

Compare the amount spent to the amount received.

Return-on-Investment beyond Financial Equivalency

The nature of the roles volunteers fill often makes it difficult to assign a monetary value to them because there is an added quality that comes from the very fact that the service is unpaid and freely given. You can hire a public relations director, but how do you calculate the worth of 100 volunteers speaking well of you out in the community? Similarly:

- Can the friendship and support of a volunteer mentor to a child be measured against the cost of a babysitter, tutor, or even an additional teacher?

- What value can you place on the hospice volunteer who supports a family while they are losing a loved one?

- How do you put a price tag on the work of the event committee members who planned the fundraiser, sold tickets to their friends, organized the entertainment, and stayed up half the night finishing the centerpieces?

- What is the full value of an updated, user-friendly Web site, designed by a volunteer, that attracts many new volunteers, clients and donors?

The Impact of *Not* Engaging Volunteers

There are costs, risks, and consequences associated with not doing something, too. So another way to assess the impact of volunteers on your organization is to consider such important questions as:

- What would be the impact on clients if the individualized attention possible from a volunteer were no longer available?

- What services might you not be able to provide and who would miss those?

- How much extra work would the staff have to do in the absence of volunteers?

- Without participation by supportive community members, would your organization have as good an image or reputation as it does? Could it count on as much word of mouth to promote your activities, solicit contributions, and find new clients?

- How could you demonstrate to potential funders that you are doing all you can to tap the resources available to you?

Four Methods of Evaluating Volunteer Involvement

Method 1:

Evaluating Quantitative Statistics

Description

Measures quantitative information about volunteer engagement, such as the number of hours of service contributed by volunteers, number of clients served, and other items that can be counted or measured. Other examples are:

- The dollar value of donated volunteer time
- Numbers of volunteers serving in different capacities within an organization
- Specifics about volunteers such as
  - Ratio of male to female volunteers
  - Approximate percentage by age group
  - Percentage by ethnicity, education, or other characteristic
  - Number employed for pay elsewhere
  - Aggregate amount of financial donations given by volunteers
  - Average length of service

Potential Benefits

- Gives you a snapshot of who is volunteering for your organization and any changes or trends compared to another time period.
- Gives you information needed for insurance purposes.
- Substantiates the monetary value you place on volunteer time.
- May help you more effectively target your recruitment message to new volunteers.

Potential Shortcomings

- The number of hours does not tell you the impact or quality of the work.
- Often, the only output or quantitative information requested is the money volunteers "saved" the organization, which is faulty reasoning because the organization did not have funds to be saved. Volunteers extend services beyond available funds.

(continued)

Four Methods of Evaluating Volunteer Involvement
(continued)

- Too often useful questions are not asked, such as:
  - Sources of new volunteers
  - Numbers of clients assisted
- There may be no resources to respond to problems that surface.

Possible Action Steps

- Increase the number of volunteers serving the organization.
- Develop a system to capture the aggregate of financial and in-kind gifts generated by current (and former) volunteers.
- Build diversity within the volunteer ranks in areas not well represented currently.
- Expand the types and quality of quantitative questions asked such as: the number of clients served by volunteers, the number of new volunteer positions developed during a specific time frame.

Method 2:

Evaluating Customer Satisfaction

Description

Asks the various constituents of volunteer involvement—which include paid staff, volunteers, executive management team, clients, funders, the community, or others—their qualitative perception of the volunteer program. The most common methods of gaining this information are through surveys, interviews, or focus group discussions.

Potential Benefits

- Satisfaction from clients greatly impacts the effectiveness and ultimate success of volunteer involvement.
- Determines the major weaknesses and strengths of volunteer involvement from the perspective of customers.
- Gains buy-in from staff for volunteer participation.
- Effectively shows appreciation for volunteers and staff.

(continued)

Four Methods of Evaluating Volunteer Involvement

(continued)

- Gathering information is easy and efficient with online survey software and reporting tools.

Potential Shortcomings

- Answers may not be truthful if there are any trust issues in the organization.

- Motivating people to respond to the survey may be challenging due to past negative experience with surveys (e.g., they took too much time, were never shared, or nothing resulted from the information collected).

- There may be no resources to respond to problems that surface.

- Satisfaction surveys measure perceptions, not necessarily reality.

Possible Action Steps

- Inform survey participants about reasons for conducting the survey and how the survey results will be used.

- Form a task force to respond to data from any survey and design action steps to respond to issues of key importance.

- Present a summary of the information/data received to those who participated and to executive staff of the organization and ask for action in response to major concerns raised.

- Provide staff training in skills of working with volunteers.

- Plan a retreat to uncover staff commitment issues and build buy-in from staff to work on diminishing staff barriers to partnering with volunteers.

- Involve volunteers in giving additional input to improve their experience as volunteers in the organization.

Method 3:

Comparing Current Effort to Accepted Standards for Leading Volunteer Engagement

Description

Compares the organization's volunteer engagement effort to external, objective management standards created by an outside body or authority.

(continued)

Four Methods of Evaluating Volunteer Involvement
(continued)

Three examples of such external standards are:

1. Canadian Code for Volunteer Involvement, http://www.volunteer. ca/en/can-code

2. Investing in Volunteers Quality Standard (UK), http://iiv.investinginvolunteers.org.uk/

3. *The Volunteer Management Audit* by Susan J. Ellis http://www.energizeinc. com/store/5-206-E-1

Potential Benefits

- Provides an education in what are considered to be excellent standards for engaging volunteers.

- Identifies areas of weakness in the program which may be impacting its effectiveness or success.

- Surfaces information that will help you develop goals for improving the program.

- Examines factors within the organization that are having an impact (positive or negative) on volunteer involvement.

Potential Shortcomings

- Requires dedication and time.

- Unhelpful and time-wasting if no action occurs after you identify areas needing improvement.

- Challenging to compare your actions to a set of generic standards.

- Overwhelming to a new leader of volunteer resources, particularly someone without training in volunteer management.

- Difficult to respond to problems that surface due to a lack of resources.

Possible Action Steps

- Identify weak areas in involving volunteers and develop a plan to improve them (e.g., if volunteers are not interviewed and screened well, develop training on the significance of interviewing and suggest key screening questions that will generate important information to consider when placing potential volunteers).

(continued)

Four Methods of Evaluating Volunteer Involvement
(continued)

- Educate key staff as to the important elements in a well-run volunteer program.

- Establish a regular system of evaluating gradual improvements in volunteer involvement (e.g., becoming more strategic and effective in recruiting, or engaging more volunteer and staff input into the designing and evaluating of volunteer participation).

Method 4:

Determining the Impact Volunteer Involvement Makes on the Mission (Outcomes-Based Evaluation)

Description

The focus of this method is on gathering qualitative information and evaluating *results*.

The main question asked is: As a result of volunteer engagement in this organization, what has changed in the lives of the clients we serve or in the mission we are trying to accomplish? (The "so-what?" question.)

Potential Benefits

- More powerful than quantitative input statistics that merely capture numbers without any indication of whether those hours given by volunteers had significant benefit to the mission of the organization.

- Provides potential funders with strong reasons for funding the organization.

- Motivates staff and volunteers because they see the results of the work they do.

- Surfaces signature stories about the impact of volunteers, which can be shared by executives during community speaking engagements.

- Helpful in determining budgetary support allocated to engaging volunteers in the future.

- Allows for measurement of specific changes in the recipients of volunteer service in such areas as:

  - Knowledge gained

  - Values altered

(continued)

Four Methods of Evaluating Volunteer Involvement

(continued)

- Behavior adjusted
- Attitude changed
- Social or economic status altered
- Skills improved
- Set goals reached
- Mood improved or stress reduced

Potential Shortcomings

- Current methods for determining impact are flawed and can be very demanding in terms of time.

- This type of evaluation can be expensive and may involve hiring a consultant (or a volunteer) to design and/or administer it.

- All components of the organization are directed at achieving the goals, making it difficult to single out and evaluate solely the impact made by volunteers.

Possible Action Steps

- Develop your organization's method of gathering and reporting on the impact of volunteer engagement.

- From information collected, develop stories about the true impact volunteers make on clients and the mission of the organization.

- Send these stories and other evaluation results to executives, board members, and funders, even when not specifically requested.

- Ask the "so what?" question about the number and ways volunteers are contributing to the organization.

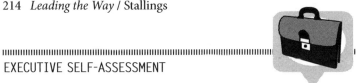

Do I monitor and evaluate volunteer involvement with these actions?

1. I expect volunteer involvement to be evaluated against stated goals and using criteria we have determined in advance.

   ☐ Yes   ☐ No   ☐ Sometimes   ☐ Will now initiate   ☐ Not relevant

2. I request that evaluation results be shared with pertinent recommendations for actions to take to address issues raised by the responses.

   ☐ Yes   ☐ No   ☐ Sometimes   ☐ Will now initiate   ☐ Not relevant

3. I expect and encourage all appropriate stakeholders to be involved in the evaluation of our organization's volunteer engagement.

   ☐ Yes   ☐ No   ☐ Sometimes   ☐ Will now initiate   ☐ Not relevant

4. I share pertinent evaluation and recommendation information with our board of directors and, if applicable, with funders and other stakeholders.

   ☐ Yes   ☐ No   ☐ Sometimes   ☐ Will now initiate   ☐ Not relevant

5. I ask for demonstration of the impact that volunteer contributions are making on the mission of our organization.

   ☐ Yes   ☐ No   ☐ Sometimes   ☐ Will now initiate   ☐ Not relevant

6. I give input to the creation of evaluation tools to be used by the leader of volunteer resources.

   ☐ Yes   ☐ No   ☐ Sometimes   ☐ Will now initiate   ☐ Not relevant

7. I give timely feedback after receiving the assessment of volunteer engagement within our organization.

   ☐ Yes   ☐ No   ☐ Sometimes   ☐ Will now initiate   ☐ Not relevant

8. I respond, as favorably as possible, to requests for additional resources needed to strengthen volunteer participation.

   ☐ Yes   ☐ No   ☐ Sometimes   ☐ Will now initiate   ☐ Not relevant

(continued)

Do I monitor and evaluate volunteer involvement with these actions?

(continued)

9. I ask for clarification of any issues, problems, or concerns that surface in the evaluation report.

    ☐ Yes   ☐ No   ☐ Sometimes   ☐ Will now initiate   ☐ Not relevant

10. I assure that we ask questions about volunteer involvement in all other evaluations we conduct on any aspect of the work of the organization.

    ☐ Yes   ☐ No   ☐ Sometimes   ☐ Will now initiate   ☐ Not relevant

Bibliography and Other Volunteerism Resources

As executive, you should expect your leader of volunteer involvement to become familiar with readily available volunteer management resources such as books, journals, Web sites and online learning, as well as become active in relevant professional associations. Of course, you may benefit from familiarizing yourself with such volunteerism resources and introducing them to board and leadership-level volunteers.

Here are some of the most commonly available sources through which to seek information on successful volunteer engagement strategies. Further information on these and other resources can be found in appendix B in *From the Top Down* (Ellis 2010, pp. 275-291).

Bibliography

There has been a steady increase in the number of publications related to volunteer management. While the following list is by no means intended to be all-inclusive or even comprehensive, it is a starting point for those learning more about the principles and practices of volunteer management.

The Energize Online Bookstore (http://www.energizeinc.com/bookstore), accompanied by its *Volunteer Management Book Blog*, offers the largest selection of titles in the field, most in electronic form. Also, on my Web site, http://www.bettystallings.com, I offer free training designs and Microsoft PowerPoint® slides as well as some of my favorite resources in volunteer management.

Campbell, Katherine Noyes, and Susan J. Ellis. (2004). *The (Help!) I-Don't-Have-Enough-Time Guide to Volunteer Management.* Philadelphia: Energize, Inc.

Connors, Tracy Daniel, ed. (1995). *The Volunteer Management Handbook.* New York: John Wiley & Sons.

Cravens, Jayne, and Susan J. Ellis. (2000). *The Virtual Volunteering Guidebook: How to Apply the Principles of Real-World Volunteer Management to Online Service.* Palo Alto, CA: Impact Online. Available for free download at http://www.energizeinc.com/download/vvguide.pdf. A revised edition is in production and expected to be available in late 2011.

Ellis, Susan J. (2010). *From the Top Down: The Executive Role in Successful Volunteer Involvement,* 3rd ed. Philadelphia: Energize, Inc.

_____. (2003). *Volunteer Management Audit.* Philadelphia: Energize, Inc.

_____. (2002). *The Volunteer (and Membership Development) Recruitment Book,* 3rd ed. Philadelphia: Energize, Inc.

Ellis, Susan J., and Katherine H. Campbell. (2005). *By the People: A History of Americans as Volunteers,* 3rd ed. Philadelphia: Energize, Inc.

Ellis, Susan J., Anne Weisbord, and Katherine H. Noyes. (2003). *Children as Volunteers: Preparing for Community Service.* Philadelphia: Energize, Inc.

Fixler, Jill Friedman, Sandie Eichberg, and Gail Lorenz. (2008). *Boomer Volunteer Engagement: Collaborate Today, Thrive Tomorrow.* Bloomington, IN: AuthorHouse.

Graff, Linda L. (2005). *Best of All: The Quick Reference Guide To Effective Volunteer Involvement.* Dundas, ON: Linda Graff and Associates.

_____. (2003). *Better Safe…Risk Management in Volunteer Programs and Community Service.* Dundas, ON: Linda Graff and Associates.

_____. (1999). *Beyond Police Checks: The Definitive Volunteer and Employee Screening Guidebook.* Dundas, ON: Linda Graff and Associates.

_____. (1997) *By Definition: Policies for Volunteer Programs,* 2nd ed. Dundas, ON: Linda Graff and Associates.

Institute for Volunteering Research. (2004). *Volunteering Impact Assessment Toolkit.* London: Volunteering England.

Kinlaw, Dennis C. (1999). *Coaching for Commitment: Interpersonal Strategies for Obtaining Superior Performance,* 2nd ed. San Francisco: Pfeiffer.

Lee, Jarene Frances, with Julia M. Catagnus. (1999). *What We Learned (the Hard Way) about Supervising Volunteers: An Action Guide to Making Your Job Easier.* Philadelphia: Energize, Inc.

Lipp, John. (2009). *The Complete Idiot's Guide to Recruiting and Managing Volunteers.* New York: Alpha (Penguin Books).

McCurley, Steve, and Rick Lynch. (2006). *Volunteer Management: Mobilizing All the Resources of the Community,* 2nd ed. Ontario, Canada: Johnstone Training and Consultation. A revised, third edition is due out late 2010.

_____. (2005). *Keeping Volunteers: A Guide to Retention.* Olympia, WA: Fat Cat Publications.

McCurley, Steve, and Sue Vineyard. (1998). *Handling Problem Volunteers: Real Solutions.* Downers Grove, IL: Heritage Arts.

Mook, Laurie, Jack Quarter, and Betty Jane Richmond. (2007). *What Counts: Social Accounting for Nonprofits and Cooperatives.* London: Sigel.

Noble, Joy, Louise Rogers, and Andy Fryar. (2010). *Volunteer Program Management: An Essential Guide,* 3rd ed. Adelaide, SA: Volunteering SA & NT.

Nonprofit Risk Management Center. (2009). *No Surprises: Harmonizing Risk and Reward in Volunteer Management,* 5th ed. Washington, DC.

Ramrayka, Liza.(2001). *Employee Volunteering: The Guide.* London: Volunteering England.

Rehnborg, Sarah Jane. (2009). *Strategic Volunteer Engagement: A Guide for Nonprofit and Public Sector Leaders.* RGK Center for Philanthropy and Community Service, The LBJ School of Public Affairs, The University of Texas at Austin.

Scheier, Ivan H. (2003). *Building Staff/Volunteer Relations.* Philadelphia: Energize, Inc.

Stallings, Betty B. (2007). *Training Busy Staff to Succeed with Volunteers: The 55-Minute Training Series.* Philadelphia: Energize, Inc.

_____. (2005). *12 Key Actions of Volunteer Program Champions: CEOs Who Lead the Way.* Philadelphia: Energize, Inc.

Valeriote, Terry. (1999). "Building Commitment for the Volunteer Program: A Replicable Model." *The Journal of Volunteer Administration,* XVII, 2: Winter 25-29.

Volunteer Vancouver. (2009). *A People Lens: 101 Ways to Move Your Organization Forward.* Vancouver, BC.

Periodicals Focused Exclusively on Volunteer Topics

- *e-Volunteerism: The Electronic Journal of the Volunteer Community,* http://www.e-volunteerism.com

- *International Journal of Volunteer Administration (IJOVA),* http://www.ijova.org

- *SALT* (Singapore), http://www.nvpc.org.sg/

- *Service Enquiry* (South Africa), http://www.service-enquiry.org.za

- *Volunteer Management Review* (published by Charity Channel), http://www.charitychannel.com/articles/article-categories/volunteer-management-review.aspx

- *Volunteering: The Magazine* (UK), http://www.volunteering.org.uk/News/volunteeringmagazine/

Online Sources of Information

Start your research at one of the "portal" Web sites listed below that collect and categorize the material for you, as well as continually adding new resources.

- **http://www.energizeinc.com.** Offers the largest Web site in the world focused exclusively on information for *leaders* of volunteers in any setting.

  With over one thousand free pages, the site hosts an extensive online library of volunteer management-related resources including articles, e-books, discussion forums, blogs, podcasts and more. You'll also find listings of volunteer-related resources around the globe, visitor-contributed quotes and stories, and much more. There is also a job bank through which you are invited to advertise any job opening for a position directly responsible for some sort of volunteer project—at no cost to you.

- **www.idealist.org.** Action Without Borders/Idealist is an international multipurpose, multilingual (English, French, and Spanish) site that serves people who wish to volunteer, agencies seeking volunteers, and people seeking jobs in either human resources or volunteer management.

- **http://www.nationalserviceresources.org.** The National Service Resource Center, administered by ETR Associates, is the knowledge management training and technical assistance provider to the Corporation for National and Community Service (commonly referred to in the field as "the Corporation").

- **http://www.volunteering.org.uk.** The Web site of Volunteering England offers a good deal of excellent information on topics as varied as corporate employee volunteering, engaging a diverse volunteer force, and more, including downloadable guides on specific subjects.

- **http://www.serviceleader.org.** ServiceLeader.org is a project of the RGK Center for Philanthropy and Community Service at The Lyndon B. Johnson School of Public Affairs of The University of Texas at Austin. It offers a range of practical and research information about volunteer management.

- **http://www.worldvolunteerweb.org.** United Nations Volunteers runs World Volunteer Web, a truly international site providing volunteer-related news and information from every country in the United Nations.

- **http://www.asaecenter.org.** The Center for Association Leadership from the American Society of Association Executives is one go-to source for leaders of membership associations, including professional societies, trade associations, and others who get their work done predominantly through the volunteer participation of their members.

- **http://www.boardsource.** BoardSource is focused exclusively on developing effective nonprofit boards of directors.

- **http://ww.taprootfoundation.org.** The Taproot Foundation is a leader in supporting corporate employee volunteering and pro bono service.

Online Discussion Forums

Just as every other profession, volunteer management has evolved ways for practitioners to exchange information and support online. Many listservs or online discussion boards exist, but three are the most established and are open to leaders of volunteers from any type of setting. CyberVPM was first and stands for "cyberspace volunteer program managers." Then came UKVPMs and OzVPM, serving the United Kingdom and Australasia, respectively. All three are hosted by Yahoo Groups and one can join by sending a blank e-mail to the following e-mail addresses:

- **cybervpm-subscribe@yahoogroups.com**
- **UKVPMs-subscribe@yahoogroups.com**
- **OzVPM-subscribe@yahoogroups.com**

For a list of other electronic discussion groups related to volunteering, see http://www.energizeinc.com/prof/listserv.html.

Volunteer Opportunity Registries

The largest of these volunteer opportunity listings in the United States are http://www.VolunteerMatch.org and http://www.Idealist.org, but there are many more, some narrowly focused on certain types of service or types of volunteers. At least thirty countries have their own online registry sites. Energize maintains a list of all such sites around the world at http://www.energizeinc.com/prof/volop.html.

Associations and Resource Providers

As an executive, you can tap available resources both to help you recruit the best leader of volunteer involvement and to offer training to your staff.

Read extensive information about the infrastructure of professional associations and volunteerism resource providers supporting effective volunteer management in appendix B in *From the Top Down*. The information there is primarily regarding the United States, but there are similar and growing infrastructures in many other countries such as Japan, Singapore, Israel, New Zealand, Australia, and across Europe.

- *At the local level*, depending on your community, there might be a volunteer center, HandsOn Action Center, or other volunteer clearinghouse that assists in connecting organizations seeking volunteers to people who want to volunteer. There may also be professional associations of leaders of volunteers, both for all types of organizations and for specialized settings or affinity groups, including corporate volunteer councils.

- *At the state or provincial level*, you may find nonprofit or government offices of volunteerism (often called "State Commissions" in the United States, if they administer federal money for national service), as well as professional associations for leaders of volunteers.

- *At the national level* there are a number of organizations and government agencies that are focused on supporting volunteerism. In the United States, the two major resources are the Corporation for National and Community Service (http://www.nationalservice.gov) and HandsOn Network/Points of

Light Institute http://www.handsonnetwork.org and http://www.pointsofli-ght.org). Throughout the world there are national bodies, such as Volunteer Canada, Volunteering England, Volunteering Australia, the National Centre for Volunteering and Philanthropy in Singapore, and many others. See the Energize Web site for a comprehensive and updated listing (http://www.ener-gizeinc.com/prof-2.html).

There are also national professional associations for leaders of volunteer involvement in many countries. For the United States, it is the Association for Leaders in Volunteer Engagement (AL!VE, http://www.volunteeralive.org).

- *At the international level* you will find United Nations Volunteers (UNV, http://www.unv.org) and the International Association for Volunteer Effort (IAVE, http://www.iave.org). There is also the European Volunteer Center (CEV, http://www.cev.be/).

Other Resource Providers in the Field

- **Council on Certification in Volunteer Administration** (CCVA, http://www. cvacert.org). Practitioners with at least three years of experience in the field of volunteer resources management can earn the credential CVA (Certified in Volunteer Administration) through this international, performance-based program.

- **The Nonprofit Risk Management Center** (http://www.nonprofitrisk.org) has produced pioneering books on volunteer risk-related subjects. The center offers a variety of online tutorials, including a volunteer risk management self-assessment tool, produces an electronic newsletter, and answers risk and insurance questions.

- **OurSharedResources.com** is an online repository of materials contributed by volunteer management practitioners for peer exchange. This site was started in 2009 by Volunteer^2 (www.volunteer2.com), Canadian developer of volunteer tracking software, and has a growing archive of downloadable, real-world examples of forms, manuals, and position descriptions, as well as templates and tools for creating resources, and more.

- In the United States, one long-standing insurance program developed to cover the unique needs of a volunteer project by providing excess accident and liability insurance is **Volunteers Insurance Service** (http://www.cima-world.com/htdocs/volunteers.cfm).

- If you are seeking volunteer tracking software, the most extensive, noneval-uative list of who is producing such software has been compiled by Jayne Cravens and can be found at her site, **Coyote Communications**, http://www. coyotecommunications.com/tech/volmanage.html.

Training and Education in Volunteer Management

There are all sorts of one-day workshops, conferences, and classes in volunteer management, sponsored by many of the organizations just identified. Energize, Inc. maintains an international listing of regularly scheduled learning opportunities as well as an international calendar of conferences and events at http://www.energizeinc.com/prof-1.html.

For Staff Who Work with Volunteers

Another critical need in professional education is developing the skills of front-line staff expected to partner with volunteers daily. These staff may be trained in any number of professions but not in the skills of working with volunteers. Here are two resources to use in teaching paid staff the fundamentals of working with volunteers in *your* setting:

- *Training Busy Staff to Succeed with Volunteers: The 55-Minute Training Series* by Betty Stallings provides twelve training modules designed for delivery in fifty-five minutes of staff time. Each electronic module comes with a complete PowerPoint® presentation; a timed script for the trainer highlighting "4 Key Concepts" on each topic; suggestions for expandable group activities; handout masters ready to duplicate, including a workshop evaluation form; and more. The complete set of modules can be purchased by individual organizations, and there are a number of limited- and unlimited-use licensing arrangements available for national organizations wishing to obtain the curriculum for their entire network. For more information, go to http://www.energizeinc.com/store/4-109-E-1 or www.bettystallings.com/bookstore.htm.

- *Everyone Ready*® is a professional development program in volunteer management delivered via online seminars, electronic self-instruction guides, interactive discussion boards, and other online resources—available to each member organization's entire network of paid and volunteer staff, 24/7 year-round. A new featured topic is presented each month, on a thirty-six month cycle. The higher the membership level, the greater the access to *Everyone Ready* resources and additional tools for each learner. Learn more at http://www.energizeinc.com/everyoneready.

About the Authors

Betty B. Stallings, MSW, is a highly regarded international trainer, keynote speaker, consultant and author specializing in volunteer management, fundraising, leadership and board development. She teaches at universities, provides training for state, national and international conferences and consults with many nonprofit organizations, public programs and foundations. Participants in her audiences and seminars note her vitality, inspiring message, engaging humor, practical presentations, and valuable resources.

For the past eighteen years, Betty has been the president of Building Better Skills whose mission is to inspire and empower people to effectively attract and utilize volunteer and financial resources to achieve their organization's mission. Her website is http://www.bettystallings.com where she gives free training resources and carries some of the best books and resources supporting volunteerism and fund development.

Betty has received numerous awards for her dedication to volunteerism and philanthropy, has previously written six books and many training curriculums and articles. Among the best-known titles are *Getting to Yes in Fundraising, Training Busy Staff to Succeed with Volunteers: The 55-Minute Staff Training Series,* and *How to Produce Fabulous Fundraising Events: Reap Remarkable Returns for Minimal Effort.* In 2005, she researched the impact of executives on successful volunteer involvement. Energize, Inc. published the results of that study in the free e-book *12 Key Actions of Volunteer Program Champions: CEOs Who Lead the Way.*

Since 2000, Betty has served as the editor/designer in charge of the "Training Designs" feature section in *e-Volunteerism: The Electronic Journal of the Volunteer Community.*

A lifelong volunteer, Betty also founded and was the fourteen-year executive director of the Valley Volunteer Center in the San Francisco Bay Area. While at the center she initiated programs which served as national models for volunteer utilization and also obtained funding and supervised innovative research on volunteer management resulting in her volunteer center's publication of the book *At the Heart—The New Volunteer Challenge to Community Agencies.*

Betty lives in Pleasanton, California, with her husband, Charles. She has two daughters and four *adorable* grandchildren! She can be reached at betty@bettystallings.com.

Susan J. Ellis is president of Energize, Inc. (http://www.energizeinc.com), an international training, consulting, and publishing firm that specializes in volunteerism. She founded the Philadelphia-based company in 1977 and since that time has assisted clients throughout the world to create or strengthen their volunteer corps.

She is the author or co-author of thirteen books, including *The Volunteer Recruitment (and Membership Development) Book, By the People: A History of Americans as Volunteers,* and *From the Top Down: The Executive Role in Successful Volunteer Involvement,* to which this book is the companion volume. She has written more than ninety articles on volunteer management for dozens of publications and writes the national bimonthly column, "On Volunteers," for *The NonProfit Times* (since 1990). In 2000, she and Steve McCurley launched the field's first online journal, *e-Volunteerism: The Electronic Journal of the Volunteer Community* (http://www.e-volunteerism.com) for which she continues to serve as editor. Susan serves as the dean of faculty for the *Everyone Ready*® online volunteer management training for organizations and individuals (http://www.energizeinc.com/everyoneready).

Made in the USA
Charleston, SC
03 September 2011